The Best M

Smith and Kraus *Books For Actors*
THE MONOLOGUE SERIES
The Best Men's / Women's Stage Monologues of 1999
The Best Men's / Women's Stage Monologues of 1998
The Best Men's / Women's Stage Monologues of 1997
The Best Men's / Women's Stage Monologues of 1996
The Best Men's / Women's Stage Monologues of 1995
The Best Men's / Women's Stage Monologues of 1994
The Best Men's / Women's Stage Monologues of 1993
The Best Men's / Women's Stage Monologues of 1992
The Best Men's / Women's Stage Monologues of 1991
The Best Men's / Women's Stage Monologues of 1990
One Hundred Men's / Women's Stage Monologues from the 1980s
2 Minutes and Under: Character Monologues for Actors
Street Talk: Character Monologues for Actors
Uptown: Character Monologues for Actors
Ice Babies in Oz: Character Monologues for Actors
Monologues from Contemporary Literature: Volume I
Monologues from Classic Plays 468 B.C. to 1960 A.D.
100 Great Monologues from the Renaissance Theatre
100 Great Monologues from the Neo-Classical Theatre
100 Great Monologues from the 19th C. Romantic and Realistic Theatres
A Brave and Violent Theatre: 20th C. Irish Monologues, Scenes & Hist. Context
Kiss and Tell: Restoration Monologues, Scenes and Historical Context
The Great Monologues from the Humana Festival
The Great Monologues from the EST Marathon
The Great Monologues from the Women's Project
The Great Monologues from the Mark Taper Forum
YOUNG ACTOR SERIES
Great Scenes and Monologues for Children
Great Monologues for Young Actors
Multicultural Monologues for Young Actors
SCENE STUDY SERIES
Scenes From Classic Plays 468 B.C. to 1970 A.D.
The Best Stage Scenes of 1999
The Best Stage Scenes of 1998
The Best Stage Scenes of 1997
The Best Stage Scenes of 1996
The Best Stage Scenes of 1995
The Best Stage Scenes of 1994
The Best Stage Scenes of 1993
The Best Stage Scenes of 1992
The Best Stage Scenes for Men / Women from the 1980s

If you require pre-publication information about upcoming Smith and Kraus books, you may receive our semi-annual catalogue, free of charge, by sending your name and address to *Smith and Kraus Catalogue, 4 Lower Mill Road, North Stratford, NH 03590. Or call us at (800) 895-4331, fax (603) 643-6431.*

The Best
Men's Stage Monologues
of 2000

edited by Jocelyn A. Beard

MONOLOGUE AUDITION SERIES

A SMITH AND KRAUS BOOK

Published by Smith and Kraus, Inc.
177 Lyme Road, Hanover, NH 03755
www.SmithKraus.com

First Edition: June 2002
10 9 8 7 6 5 4 3 2 1

cover illustration by Lisa Goldfinger
cover and text design by Julia Hill Gignoux

The Monologue Audition Series
ISSN 1067-134X
ISBN 1-57525-288-0

CONTENTS

Dedicated to the Victims of September 11, 2001

AFTER DARWIN
Timberlake Wertenbacker

Scene: A room, 30 April 1865. 7 A.M.
Dramatic
Robert FitzRoy, (forty to fifty), Captain of *The Beagle*. A man confronting his
philosophical nemesis.

*Here FitzRoy, a devout Christian, confronts Charles Darwin, the man he es-
corted on the naturalist's great adventure.*

FITZROY: This is the truth. 'Woe unto thee, blind guide . . .' Natural selec-
tion? We cannot survive without The Book. You want a grim future, without purpose, mockery of all that is sacred, no moral light. 'It had been
better for that man if he had not been born.' I harboured you in my cabin.
I, FitzRoy of *The Beagle*, have brought destruction on the world — 'Woe
unto that man by whom the offense cometh.' That nose, that nose, why
did I tear up the letter? *(Pause.)* I only ever wanted to do what was right.
I understood it, it was my inheritance — but perhaps there is no right,
no good. Forgive me, God, for what I have done, for what I'm about to
do — if you are there.
(He brandishes the razor at Darwin, who does not react.)
You were the mediocrity, I had the destiny — you scrambled my destiny,
and the world. *(He turns away.)* Perhaps God never looked. The fittest,
so-called, grimacing their success. Thousands like you in this world sod-
den with vulgarity. No more like me. They laugh at me. No more now.
I leave nothing behind. *(To Darwin.)* But you never saw the pain of ex-
tinction. *(He draws the razor up to his throat to slit it.)*

ALL ABOUT DOC
Christopher Woods

Scene: Here and now
Dramatic
Man (thirties) who has just committed a terrible act.

Here, a man recounts the chiling events that led to murder.

(A redneck, wearing a bloody apron, drinks a beer.)

MAN: Sure, I'll admit it. No problem. We weren't so smart. Now, it's different. But last night, I guess we didn't know no better. Clint and me. That's
why we went ahead with it. The project. Yeah, that's what we called it.
THE PROJECT. *(Chuckles.)*

Doc, he'd been our neighbor awhile. We counted on him for the wisdom business. And vodka, too, when we was out. Doc, he was real smart.
But he'd been out of his line of work a long time. But that don't mean
he didn't like to talk about it. He did.

I'd ask him, "Doc, how do you crack one?" We'd be drinking boil-
ermakers. And Doc, he said it was like cracking some old dinosaur egg.
Kinda hard, you see. He even showed us how to do it. He pulled out that
black doctor bag, the one he hadn't used in so long? He blew off the dust.
He showed us his shiny tools. He'd been sidelined a few years for shaky
hands and what all.

After he got everything spread out on the kitchen table, I asked him
how he knew what was what. So he told me. He got out some big old
book. Doc showed me a map of the brain. Like a roadmap, but all the
roads was inside, if you follow me.

I was watchin' Doc, looking at the pictures. That's close as he'd got
to operatin' again, least 'til he got his hands settled down. But there wasn't
much chance of that happening, the way Clint and me saw it. No, Doc
was down the tubes. Else why was he hangin' 'round with a couple guys
like us?

That roadmap book was the first thing I went lookin' for last night
in Doc's kitchen. When things went wrong? And Clint acting like a yellow bastard, lettin' me do all the work. Oh, he helped me to crack Doc's

dinosaur egg, but that was only after I started hollerin' at him.

Once I had everything all out on the table, I started lookin' at it real hard. And you know what? Doc's brains didn't look like the ones in the book. No roadmap, is what I mean. Messier, too.

I didn't let that stop me. I'd look at Doc's brains, then the pictures in the book. I started seein' things. Places I didn't know about before. I came across the place where feelings hole up. And this and that, like where talk starts. I poked around. There wasn't no labels or nothin' like in the book. No, it was more like pushin' jelly 'round on a plate.

While I'm doin' this, Clint's walkin' 'round the kitchen. Openin' cabinets, then slammin' them shut. He's bitchin' 'cause he can't find Doc's gin bottle. He was so drunk he couldn't stand up straight. I said, Clint, you dumb fucker, how do you think we got Doc to pass out in the first place? We got Doc to drink that whole bottle. Good thing, too. Who can have their head split open without some of that . . . oh, what you call it? Uh, yeah, *annis asia*. That's what it's called.

I'm working hard, see? And Clint, he's breakin' out the bourbon. Sour mash. I say, give me some of that stuff. Settle my stomach with all that blood everywhere. Doc's brains was pretty good for browsing. I was enjoying myself. I told myself I was. Pretty soon, though, it wasn't fun anymore. Things started dryin' out on the table. *Real dry.* I knew my time was runnin' out. I tried to put it all back like I found it. Like in the book?

But I looked at all that flattened out jelly, and I didn't know the first thing 'bout puttin' it back together. Oh, I tried to line it all up nice and proper. Clint was watchin'. I knew he was thinkin' the same thing.

Clint said he didn't recall me askin' Doc about this part. That's what I know, I said. That's what I know. Damned if it wasn't so! I just forgot to ask. *(Beat.)* Hell knows it was too late to ask Doc.

So maybe I messed up big time. Wouldn't you say so? Yeah. How else can you explain how somethin' like this happens. *(Beat.)* I'm gonna study Doc's book real hard. Next time, I'll be ready. *(Blackout.)*

AM LIT
or Hibernophobia
Dan O'Brien

Scene: Here and now
Serio-Comic
Joe (forty to fifty), a man reconnecting with the past.

Here, a college professor writes a letter to a woman and a country who both changed his life forever.

JOE: Katherine Sullivan, 35 Presentation Ave., off Cathedral Road, Cork City, IRELAND:

Kate.

Remember me?

I remembered you today. Going through some old box and what should I find but you? — a picture of you — you and me in Cobh. (Site of the sinking of the *Lusitania*.) An Italian tourist took it. That statue of the emigrants leaving Ireland behind, pointing out across the ocean towards New York: In the picture I have my right nostril hooked onto the pointing, sculpted finger of a famine victim. You are laughing gorgeously.

What is it about that country? your country, I mean — Ireland. All these years, I can't seem to get it out of my mind . . .

I remember, when I came home — what was it?, twenty-five, -six years ago? (Jesus Christ! Jesus!) — anyway, and I got that scorching case of mono and the nurse was taking blood and she could see I was about to pass out from the sight of it, and she said:

"Do you think the Irish are the soul of literature?" (She knew where I'd been.)

Well I couldn't answer, you see; I'd already passed out.

But the point is I think they are: I think you are: The soul of literature. You will say I am just being romantic. You always said I was a hopeless romantic.

— I can't believe I'm writing this.

I've wanted to write you a hundred times — thousands. But each time I got a page in I said, Now who am I writing to? Who?

You know what I mean, Kate?

So how've you been?

Someone once told me you got married, I forget who. Connor, I think? I saw him in Boston in the snow on a streetcorner years ago. Do you see him much anymore?

I got married, too.

And I'm writing because I've been thinking, Kate:

About Ireland, but not all the hokey stuff, the bogs and the pints and dog shite in the sidewalk, but things like the weather, like walking through Cork City like a beehive with you in a very light warm rain, or the sweet burnt smell of hops and barley lying fat like fog in the gutter off South Main, or that moon in April when we drove all the way out to Blarney Castle because I'd told you, I'd told you I'd liked you and you said you liked me too and what else could we do but drive out to the country, and pull over in the weeds and kiss, and talk, and make love, your face like touching a mirror —

I swear I'm not being romantic.

I'm not drunk, either.

I don't write poetry anymore; I'm a college professor now.

And I'm writing to you because I'm leaving America, for good. I'm coming back to Ireland. And I'd very much like to see you again, if you're free —.

AN EMPTY PLATE IN THE CAFE
DU GRAND BOEUF

Michael Hollinger

Scene: A cafe in Paris, July 1961
Serio-Comic
Victor (fifties), a big bull of a man attempting an unusual suicide.

> *Brokenhearted Victor has decided to starve himself to death. His first port of call is the Cafe du Grand Boeuf, a gormand's paradise. Here, he muses on the concept of abundance with a befuddled headwaiter.*

VICTOR: Ah, *abundance*, well. There's a deceptive word. Abundance is never about what you have. It's about what you can't have, ever.

[CLAUDE: What?]

VICTOR: And never's such a long, long time. Imagine yourself in the Garden of Eden and somebody tells you that you can have anything. Anything! *Except* one little apple. You didn't even want an apple, but now you can't have it, and it occupies your mind. You can't stop thinking about it, even while you're sleeping. Especially then. And pretty soon you don't want mangos, or quinces, or chicken Tetrazzini, or anything else you've got in *abundance,* you want that apple. And anything less is hell.

[GASTON: I've got a nice apple in the back —]

VICTOR: *(Increasing in intensity.)* Or consider a worm in a bottle of tequila. He should be ecstatic: he's got all the tequila he can drink, lucky worm. *But he doesn't want tequila, does he?*

AN EMPTY PLATE IN THE CAFE DU GRAND BOEUF

Michael Hollinger

Scene: A cafe in Paris, July 1961
Serio-Comic
Victor (fifties), a big bull of a man attempting an unusual suicide.

Here, Victor shares a memory of Ernest Hemingway with the denizens of the cafe.

VICTOR: He wasn't cleaning his shotgun; he was cleansing his palate.

[MIMI: Eew.]

VICTOR: Do you honestly think a man who shot leopards, elephants, and enemy soldiers in two world wars would empty a twelve-gauge shell in his head by accident? Isn't it more likely he just wanted to get the sour taste of life out of it once and for all?

[MIMI: But who's to say he's better off now?]

VICTOR: I met him once. Here, just after the Liberation, at the Hotel Ritz. Drinking an absinthe and dissecting a revolver on the table like he was eating crabs. A reporter from Chicago introduced us. Hemingway turned around in his chair and took me in, half closing his eyes as if he wanted to see what I was really made of. Then he nodded and grinned with that big, warm Hemingway smile. But before he turned away, he said something to me I've never forgotten, even after all these years. He said, "You've got dog shit on your shoes." He was right; I did. I left the hotel to scrape them off, and when I came back he was gone.

(He takes his newspaper back.)

Now tonight some pimple-faced son of a publisher empties his obit file to summarize the man in fifty column inches. Makes his deadline, too. He just has to leave out his whole damn life and stick with who-what-where-when-why. *(To Antoine.)* You getting all this?

ANTON IN SHOW BUSINESS
Jane Martin

Scene: San Antonio, Texas
Serio-Comic
Joe Bob (forty to fifty), an artistically-challenged conservative.

Here, the rancorous Joe Bob fires Kate, whose only crime was to try and bring theatre to San Antonio.

JOE BOB: *(From somewhere out in the house.)* Damn woman! You got no more sense than a hog on ice! I have been pourin' my money an' the money of my friends down your double-talk rathole since Jesus was a pup, so my wife could drag me down here to see plays nobody can understand with a buncha people I would never invite to dinner, on the basis it creates some quality of life I'm supposed to have since I figgered out how to make some money. Half the time, that stuff doesn't have a story, and it's been five years since you done one takes place in a kitchen, which is the kind all of us like. The rest of the time it's about how rich people is bad and Democrats is good and white people is stupid and homosexuals have more fun an' we should get rid of the corporations an' eat grass an' then, by God, you wonder why you don't have a big audience? Now you just blew 15% of your budget 'cause you riled up the tobacco interests, plus you got the colored rattlin' on my cage, an' then, by God, we can go back to hittin' each other up to give to the United Way where it will, by God, do some poor handicap some actual, measurable good, an' I won't have to hear anybody say "aesthetic" from one year to the goddamned next! Now, vaya con Dios, darlin'.

APARTMENT 3A
Jeff Daniels

Scene: A city of some size in the Midwest
Dramatic
Elliot (thirties), a man considering his faith and his place in the universe.

Elliot and Annie have been dancing around a relationship but spiritual matters have driven a slight wedge between them. Here, Elliot confesses a lapse of faith and a subsequent encounter with the spirit world.

ELLIOT: I lied.

[ANNIE: What?]

ELLIOT: *(Unemotional.)* When I told you I never had doubts. I have. True story. Both my parents died when I was young. My father went first. My mother lasted until I was fifteen. Cancer. Boom, she had it. Boom she was gone. There was almost no time to take it in. My brother and I went to live with my grandparents. Very Catholic. Which was good because we were kind of lost. Alone, except for each other. And I remember thinking, where did she go? The priest told me she was in heaven because God needed her, and I remember telling him, "Yeah, but I need her more." And that was the first time I thought that maybe there wasn't any heaven. Or a God. At least one I would want to be with. I mean, He took my mother away from me. And I told my brother and he said he didn't believe in heaven anymore either, but that he still believed in angels. And mom was an angel. That way she could still be alive. At least in his head. And I said, "Yeah, but if there's no heaven, where do the angels go? Do they just fly around forever or what?" And we didn't really have an answer for that. Anyway, we turned out okay, the both of us. He's down in Fort Wayne now, running his own supermarket. Wife, four kids, house, y'know. And then about two years ago, I was asleep one night and I had this dream where I saw her. I saw my mom. She sat right on the edge of my bed, looking at me. And I sat up. Hugged her. And I could feel her. I could actually smell her. And then she talked to me. Asked me how I was doing. If I was okay. And I told her I was fine but that I missed her and she said she missed me, too, and that she was glad I hadn't forgotten her. And then I woke up. And I sat there in the middle of the night, bawling my eyes out because I could still smell her. Feel her. Few weeks later, I saw my brother. Told him about it. And he said, "Oh, my God," and started crying. And I said, "What? What is it?" and he said, "I had the same exact dream two weeks ago." . . . Now, I don't know if that proves anything. But it happened. Weird, huh?

APERTURA MODOTTI

Ellen Gavin

Scene: Spain
Serio-Comic
George Orwell (forty to fifty), the author, a rumpled idealist.

Here, the author of 1984 *and* Animal Farm *remembers his time in Spain fighting in the Spanish Civil War.*

ORWELL: George Orwell here. *Animal Farm? 1984?* Hey, you lived through it, which is more than I can say!
(Aside.)
Didn't it scare the bejeezus outta you to have all of that hanging over your head . . . *newspeak, doublethink,* no decent sex . . .
Well you survived, I hope. Just tried to warn you where the mind could go with no attachments. With no responsibility to history . . . to . . .
(He is straightening the books on his messy desk, in search of his glasses.)
. . . *Ideas* . . . to . . . *ideals.* When you're young you think these are all you need to change the world. *(He continues searching.) Ideas. Ideals.* They had their power then, they have it now. But what youth doesn't take into account is another kind of power. The old, unabashed, cynical power of force. From the right. Or the left.
(Orwell realizes his glasses are sitting on top of his head. He finds them, puts them on his nose, cloudy and crooked.)
Spain was our Nicaragua. (Nec-a-RAG-ua). The Spanish Civil War was our line in the sand. An' when you're risking your one and only life on a battlefield . . . you'd think these things'd stay straight, right?
Communism, anarchism, freedom, democracy: OUR SIDE. Fascism and totalitarianism, on the other side with the Spanish Falange, Hitler's Nazis, Mussolini's Blackshirts and . . .
England, France and the United States?
That's right. Nothing new. On the wrong side in Spain, too. When exactly has the United States been on the right side of history?

ARCTIC QUEST
Linda Stockham

Scene: Somewhere in the Arctic Circle, 1900
Dramatic
Andrew Williams (thirty-eight), an early 20th-century arctic explorer

In 1900, Andrew, a physician, joined a doomed balloon expedition to the North Pole. Stranded, lost and dying, he here remembers the many things that influenced his departure.

ANDREW: The silent activity of the fog moves along like a snail pulling a great curtain behind it.

There hides the unhallowed ice — a deceitful angel, beckoning safety in its outstretched arms — Blake's "fiend hid in a cloud"* It is a gray, bleak, and dangerous fog!

(He regains an impression of calmness.)

There is no *Open Polar Sea;* there is no temperate oasis to offer sanctuary. There is only death. And as a physician I know too well that death awaits us all. It is always there, from the moment of our conception; it is always there, the guide into the hereafter — whereever that might me. And as a physician, I am ashamed of my innocent, egotistic stupidity when it came to the careless way I set out to reach the North Pole. I defied reason; I failed to see anything but the glory of the quest.

But I was not alone — for others were the same in a quest of glory. The adventurer always pursues this dream. Oh, not all, of course. Not all. My wife, usually a self-contained woman, saw through my motives. "I might be obsessed with being the first known human to reach the North Pole," she said, "but I wasn't going after that dream for any other reason than to be the first known human to go there." I see her sitting at home refusing to mourn my death and to laugh at my idiocy about my trek to the North Pole. A practical woman; however, she most surely is not a woman to undercut any ambitions of mine but at the same time, not one to bestow approval. But I had to remind her when this expedition was in its infant stage that I had for thirty-eight years been quite the contented physician, husband, and father. Now I wanted to free myself of those years and pursue my dream.

(He laughs quietly.)

"To pursue my dream"? she had questioned. "Well, you can go to your death, Andrew, but I shall be satisfied to endeavor the known heat of summer in Indianapolis than the unknown freezing hardship of the Arctic." And she said no more about my expedition and upon the day of my departure, she did not see me off. Rather, she left the house before me to go about her regular routine of visiting our married daughter and calling upon a childhood friend of hers before going about her church work. In fact, she is probably as busy with her regular routine of day-to-day living as I am hearing the faint echoes of her judgmental remarks. But such is the yoke of guilt that wives can place upon men who dream of things apart from that simple day-to-day sense of life.

(Sternly and emphatically.)

I had my thirty-eight years of responsibility. I wanted my time of adventure.

(Quietly and perhaps less resolved now.)

What do women know of adventure? What do they know of a man's need to escape his known world and discover ones new to him? What do they know of the ambitious dreams of Jason, Odysseus, and Captain Cook? What do they know of the greater glory of being the first . . . the great glory of adventure?

Infant Sorrow. [Public Domain.]

ARCTIC QUEST
Linda Stockham

Scene: Somewhere in the Arctic Circle, 1900
Dramatic
Andrew Williams (thirty-eight), an early 20th-century arctic explorer

Here, Andrew recalls the crash of the balloon and the trick of fate that caused their deaths.

ANDREW: Balloons sore as dreams float upon tranquil summer airs. Foolish men who do not prepare for the unexpected all too soon become the prey of their own aspirations.

There is no way to know how close we came to the North Pole. All we can say, upon our crash, is that we were out of Virgo Harbor but a day and a night before the Chinese pongee silk was ripped by an abrupt swell of the wind from the south. The gondola and balloon hit an ice pack, but the rest slipped into a watery crack in the ice — lost and silent in a frigid abyss.

(Bemused underscoring.)

Such is a desolate world full of danger and obliteration.

(Marking the spot in a glance.)

We came down here, lost somewhere beyond Virgo Harbor. It is here that we finally understood the nature of the place and our Fate. And it is here that we met the white monster. It arose out of the whiteness; it emerged from the snow like a supernatural being. It took form; it stood on its hind legs like an evil demon; and it attacked without conscious. And like that terrified deer that saw the death my grandfather was bringing it, I froze.

(He picks up the chisel-head hammers.)

But Sam Keck, with his usual vibrato, grabbed two chisel-head hammers from the gondola and ran up the back of the Polar bear, and with all of his might, he thrust the blades into the eyes of the bear. As the bear cried out terrifying screams of surprise and pain, it released its deadly grip on Josiah. At the moment when Josiah fell to the ground, Sam jumped from the back of the bear to pull him to safety. It was then that Sam yelled at me, for I still remained trapped in catalytic terror. Twice more he yelled out my name, and twice more I stood there, unable to run away from the screaming white monster before me. It was reeling there a few feet from me; its front paws clawing at the hammers in his eyes. The blood was flowing down across his muzzle, to his neck, underside, hind legs, and staining the snow around his back paws. Then it came down on all fours, rolling its face in the snow, trying to rid itself of the hammers and the pain.

(He retrieves the rifle.)

I watched the bear fall into the snow as Sam moved forward with the rifle from the gondola. He shot it twice in the head, silencing the screaming but also the pounding of its heart. It collapsed to one side, and seeing its blood stained face, I saw our Fate!

(He sets the rifle aside.)

Josiah died a few hours later of internal hemorrhaging. The bear had crushed his insides within the few minutes that it had locked him in its predatorial embrace. There was nothing I could do.

(He picks up the logbook.)

We wrapped Josiah's body in part of the airship's gasbag and did our best to carve out a grave in the snow. Then Sam took to cutting out some meat from the bear. We ate it raw; there was nothing else we could do. I had had bear meat before, as a child. Sam had not and wasn't particularly keen on it but our food supplies went into the sea when the *Arctic Quest* crashed. And our crude fishing lines into the water failed realization of any fish, which would have been more appetizing than the raw, tough meat of the Polar bear. It was as Sam carved out portions for us and we started eating it that we concluded that it was an old bear. And as we gnawed almost painfully on the meat, we decided that no manner of cooking, if we had the ability to build a fire, would have done much to ease its toughness. And in the end, the Polar bear would beat us out . . . in a secret, ancient ritualism that only Fate controls.

The irony is that as a medical doctor I should have known . . . But not until Sam died did I recognize what it was that brought on our fever, muscle weakness, and death. It came from the Polar bear — *Trichinosis*. I had seen it throughout my career as a doctor. In most cases, the felon was pork.

History, if I should be remembered for this ill-fated attempt to fly to the North Pole, will see me not as a glorious adventurer but a stupid, incompetent fool who set out to conquer Nature but was instead conquered by Nature.

(He crosses up to the gondola.)

My Fate.

(He holds up the logbook.)

Let it lie within the tomb of disenchantment.

(He stuffs logbook inside his coat.)

Let these pages bind to the bones of this fool.

(He pivots and looks up into the sky.)

Sometimes I hear a bird singing; it is a lost, forgotten bird.

(To the audience.)

It is a sad, joyous song breaking down from a high place in the sky. A beckoning call falling from out of time.

(He tightens his coat about him.)

The ice floe is a desert; it freezes the blood and laughs cracklingly at human defeat. My dream — the mirage of a lost *Saharan* wayfarer. There, before me. Illusive.

Taunting. An oasis never to be reached. A haven never to be encountered.

(He moves downstage center, to the very edge of the stage's apron.)

Let it go — Let it float away into the fog that cloaks this *Hadean* world of snow and ice.

(He reaches out to grasp what slips away into darkness.)

Gone.

BACK STORY
What Became of the Polar Bear?
Mayo Simon

Scene: The home of Herman Melville, Pittsfield, Massachusetts
Serio-Comic
Ethan (eighteen), a tour guide.

Here, Ethan tells his tour group the story of what inspired Melville to write
Moby-Dick.

ETHAN: In the summer of 1850, Herman Melville, seeking a quiet place to
work, bought this eighteenth-century farmhouse in the town of Pittsfield,
which was then home to such famous literary figures as Fanny Kemble,
Oliver Wendell Holmes, James Russell Lowell, and in Lenox, less than
six miles away, Nathaniel Hawthorne. I can repeat that in German. Spanish? French? Serbo-Croatian? Okay, everybody into Herman's study. If you
look out the window you can see — Mount Greylock! You'll notice the
top of the mountain is shaped like the head of a huge whale. This is the
view, ladies and gentlemen, that became the inspiration for Melville's great-
est novel, *Moby-Dick!*
(Quietly.)
If you believe that, you'll believe anything. Now, you want to hear the
real story of how Melville got the idea for *Moby-Dick?*
(Motions people to gather around him.)
They don't like me to talk about this — too controversial. But you've been
such a good group . . .
(Looks around, then continues.)
Herman Melville was a harpooner on a whaling ship for two years. Started
in the South Seas, ended up in the Gulf of Alaska. One foggy morning,
as the ship is maneuvering around the ice floes where the whales hang
out, Melville spies what's left of a fishing boat. Whales get a kick out of
ramming boats, so Herman's on the lookout. Sure enough, coming out
of the fog, he sees something. It's not a whale. It's a man . . . on an ice
floe . . . fishing. Name's Belcher — same name as mine — common name.
And on that floe is also . . . a polar bear. Melville hails the man: "Avast,

have you seen a great white whale?" They look at each other, Melville the harpooner, and Belcher, owner and manager of Belcher Electric. Then, as though he's come to some secret and profound conclusion about life, the man raises his arms and . . . takes off! Actually, a huge whale has crashed up from under the ice, lifting the man high in the air. Melville watches as the whale, with a giant splash, flops down in the water. The man flops down on the whale's back. The whale, with Belcher on his back, dives into the fog and disappears. Awesome. Melville is too stunned to throw the harpoon. Instead, he decides to write a book. It's all in one of Melville's letters to Hawthorne. You can look it up. What's that? What became of the polar bear? Strange you should ask because I ask the same question every night . . . What became of him? . . . That concludes the tour. The gift shop is down the steps and to the right.

BIG LOVE
Charles L. Mee

Scene: A country torn apart by war.
Dramatic
Constantine (twenty to thirty), a man confronting a runaway bride.

Thyona has been promised to Constantine since before they were born. When she rejects the notion of an arranged marriage, he pursues her and makes the following declaration.

CONSTANTINE: What do you think?
    You think you live in a world nowadays where
    you can throw out a promise
    just because you don't feel like keeping it?
    Just because
    drugs are rife
    gambling is legal
    medicine is euthanasia
    birth is abortion
    homosexuality is the norm
    pornography is piped into everybody's home on the internet
    now you think you can do whatever you want
    whenever you want to do it
    no matter what the law might say?
    I don't accept that.
    Sometimes I like to lie down at night
    with my arms around someone
    and KNOW she is there for me
    know this gives her pleasure —
    my arms around her
    her back to me
    my stomach pressed against her back
    my face buried in her hair
    one hand on her stomach
    feeling at peace.
    That's my plan

to have that.
I'll have my bride.
If I have to have her arms tied behind her back
and dragged to me.
I'll have her back.
What is it you women want
you want to be strung up with hoods and gags and blindfolds
stretched out on a board with weights on your chest
you want me to sew your legs to the bed
and pour gasoline on you
and light you on fire
is that what I have to do to keep you?

BIG LOVE
Charles L. Mee

Scene: A country torn apart by war.
Dramatic
Constantine (twenty to thirty), a man confronting a runaway bride.

*Here, angry Constantine ruminates on how difficult it can be to be a man
in a world ruled by violence.*

CONSTANTINE: People think
    it's hard to be a woman;
    but it's not easy
    to be a man,
    the expectations people have
    that a man should be a civilized person
    of course I think everyone should be civilized
    men and women both
    but when push comes to shove
    say you have some bad people
    who are invading your country
    raping your own wives and daughters
    and now you see:
    this happens all the time
    all around the world
    and then a person wants a man
    who can defend his home
    you can say, yes, it was men who started this
    there's no such thing as good guys and bad guys
    only guys
    and they kill people
    but if you are a man who doesn't want to be a bad guy
    and you try not to be a bad guy
    it doesn't matter
    because even if it is possible to be good
    and you are good
    when push comes to shove

and people need defending
then no one wants a good guy any more
then they want a man who can fuck someone up
who can go to his target like a bullet
burst all bonds
his blood hot
howling up the bank
rage in his heart
screaming
with every urge to vomit
the ground moving beneath his feet
the earth alive with pounding
the cry hammering in his heart
like tanked up motors turned loose
with no brakes to hold them

this noxious world

and then when it's over
suddenly
when this impulse isn't called for any longer
a man is expected to put it away
carry on with life
as though he didn't have such impulses
or to know that, if he does
he is a despicable person
and so it may be that when a man turns this violence on a woman
in her bedroom
or in the midst of war
slamming her down, hitting her,
he should be esteemed for this
for informing her
about what it is that civilization really contains
the impulse to hurt side by side with the gentleness
the use of force as well as tenderness
the presence of coercion and necessity
because it has just been a luxury for her really

not to have to act on this impulse or even feel it
to let a man do it for her
so that she can stand aside and deplore it
whereas in reality
it is an inextricable part of the civilization in which she lives
on which she depends
that provides her a long life, longer usually than her husband,
and food and clothes
dining out in restaurants
and going on vacations to the oceanside
so that when a man turns it against her
he is showing her a different sort of civilized behavior really
that she should know and feel intimately
as he does
to know the truth of how it is to live on earth
to know this is part not just of him
but also of her life
not go through life denying it
pretending it belongs to another
rather knowing it as her own
feeling it as her own
feeling it as a part of life as intense as love
as lovely in its way as kindness
because to know this pain
is to know the whole of life
before we die
and not just some pretty piece of it
to know who we are
both of us together
this is a gift that a man can give a woman.

THE BRONX HEBREW
SCHOOL AND SPORTS BOOK
Rooster Mitchell

Scene: The Bronx, 1930s
Serio-Comic
Lou (forty to fifty), director of the Bronx Hebrew School.

Here, Lou plans the yearly school seder while demanding that it be better than last year's.

LOU: We do it right or we don't do it. Last year's debacle. Fucked it up so bad, brings tears to my eyes.

For starters, someone, won't mention names, *you,* neglected to bring grape juice in for the Kiddush; instead, we had two cases of cheap wine pulled out of the wine cellar polished off by the kids in a matter of two hours. A room full of bombed, belligerent children is not so responsible.
(Beat.)
Real wine; bad, runny charoses, dry turkey, kids vomiting all over each other, breaking out in hives. All this, and somebody, won't mention names, *you,* forgot the fucking horseradish, the bitter herbs! I ask you, how can you have a legitimate seder without the bitter herbs? This was not a seder; it was a sham, a punch-in-the-nose to Judaism. You think kids don't talk? They talk. *Boy* do they talk. They go home *drunk* and tell their parents they had dry turkey and no fucking bitter herbs! I'm still getting calls. We have a reputation, understand?

. . . see that you don't fuck up this year. Find a new caterer, one with integrity. When he prepares this meal for a hundred-plus children, I want you to stand over his fucking shoulder, make sure his charoses is thick not runny, full of red apples. Taste it with a fork. You know how it should taste; like your grandmother usta make God rest her sweet soul. If it's runny force him to make it thicker. Make sure it meets all of your specifications right down to the proper allotment of raisins and lemon squeezings. Now the *turkey:*
(Beat.)
The turkey should be moist and tender, not like last year's *drek.* If you

taste the food and still think it's not up to snuff, and he refuses to improve on it, notify me immediately and I will gladly make a phone call to have his fucking hands broken to where he never holds another spatula; do you understand these things?

. . . good, because I am, for the love of God, *counting* on you to come through for me . . . First off, what I'll need you to do is go to Manny's on 10th and price some new Haggadahs . . . Ones we have now've been sat on, chewed on, spit on, and so on. As for the seder plate —

. . . last year the help made off with it. The fucking help! Believe that shit?! I swear to Christ and five other unshaven white men, I catch the low-lifes who stole our seder plate, *forget about it.* Sonsabitches. Buy a new one, ya hear? . . . nice one, with little pictures of each food item. The egg, the parsley, the shank —

Now listen to me: for the singing of the "Four Questions" we'll have a *talent* contest. Last year we bestowed the honor on Sherman "Shoe-licker" Mendelson based on his essay, and he turns around and fucks it up. Turned a holy prayer into a comedy routine. No friggin' essays this year, got that?

. . . good. Now don't be a jackass this year, hear me? No fucking booze. Grape juice, remember? These kids get plastered again, I *assure* you, we're gonna get pinched.

No, that is not all. When you make the seating arrangement, make sure little Albert Tennanbaum sits nowheres near Melissa Greenberg. Guy's got a boner the size a' Staten Island for this broad. And keep Benny Borowitz away from the cake, the fat pig. And last but not least, Chris*sake*, when you hide the Afikoman, hide it where it can be found. Last year, you hid it where it can be found. Last year, you hid it in the fucking ceiling tiles. Just out of curiosity, what the hell were you thinking? —

(As Jake starts to answer.)

. . . nevermind . . . I don't tell you these things now I swear on your Bubby's blue eyes you'll sleep right through the fucking thing. Seder. Food. Jews need to be entertained . . . That's it, oughta keep you busy, yes?

COASTER
Adam Langer

Scene: Chicago
Serio-Comic
Cal (twenty to thirty), a maker of Italian Ice.

When his business is called "Chicago's worst Italian Ice" by a critic in the press, Cal explodes with fury and prepares to leave for greener pastures.

CAL: Not so good, man.

[SAM: *(To Dr. Waters.)* There was a FOR RENT sign out front.]

CAL: Not so good.

[SAM: No business?]

CAL: No fucking business. No fucking respect. You know what I mean, man? You take your life. You take your whole life, man and people, you know, they just take it as something to laugh at. Ha ha, he makes shit Italian Ice, so what, another asshole trying to make a living —that's all I am — just another asshole trying to make a living. If people got a problem, I don't got a problem. They can come to me with their problem, but then they wanna write shit about you, not come to you face-to-face like an honest fucking person, not come in talk about it man to man. All I'm trying to do, give people something they want, put a smile on a kid's face. They don't wanna buy it, they don't gotta buy it, fuck it, man. I don't like eating *normal* Italian Ice. I don't like fucking Lemon. I don't like Grape. I don't like fucking Piña Colada, show you how out of touch with the rest of the universe I fucking am. What kind of price do I gotta pay for that. Some asshole's ridicule? I don't gotta take that shit. That's not part of the motherfucking job description. Go to fucking hell, go eat fucking LEMON, don't be a leader; be a joiner. Hell, I don't care. I ain't vindictive. There's no fucking place in this town for creative fucking people. Anybody in this world who comes from this place also winds up being somebody go one fucking place and you know where that is? That's Madison Fucking Wisconsin. So stop pushing me. I now where I gotta be. And if I weren't a religious man, if I wasn't a God-fearing pilgrim — cause that's who we all are, man, all God's little fucking pilgrims — I'd tell that writer asshole, that scrawny little piece of . . . poised behind his little piece of shit IMAC that I put $50,000 doubloons into this business, that he ruined a man's livelihood and shat on his self-respect. But I'm better than that and I'm better off knowing I'm better than him however much I lost. But that's the game. The last thing I want to be known as is vindictive, so fuck him. He's an asshole. I'm off to Madison Fucking Wisconsin and Chicago can suck my dick.

DINNER WITH FRIENDS
Donald Margulies

Scene: Here and now
Serio-Comic
Tom (late thirties to forty), a man whose marriage is in crisis.

Here, Tom complains to his best friend about his deteriorating sex life with his wife and his decision to have an affair with his travel agent.

TOM: I don't know about you, but I'm at the point in my life where I want to enjoy myself. I don't want to go through life hoping I'm gonna get lucky with my own *wife*. You know? You go to bed and you think you're gonna have sex and then you say something, some kind of offhanded remark of no consequence whatsoever, and it pisses her off and the mood is gone and it's lights out and that's it. I must've masturbated more than any married man in history.

[GABE: I doubt that. Besides, who ever said marriage meant sex twenty-four hours on demand?]

TOM: I'm not asking for it twenty-four hours a day, all I'm asking for is a little affection. *(Gabe nods. Pause.)*

[GABE: Have there been other women?]

TOM: *(Offended.)* No!

[GABE: Sorry.]

TOM: No, Gabe, there were no other women. There *were* opportunities, though. I mean, when you're out of town as much as *I* am . . . You're lonely, you're far from home, it doesn't seem like you're living in real time. I'd be in a hotel bar and strike up a conversation with a female colleague, or some divorcee with big hair, and I'd make them laugh and they'd look pretty and I'd feel competent again, you know?, and think, Gee, maybe I *am* still clever and attractive after all. There'd be that electricity in the air, that kind of buzz I hadn't felt since college, remember?, when a single move, any move at all, and there'd be sex? But I'd get scared and say goodnight and go back to my room and call Beth out of guilt, or hope, and get some shit about something I neglected to do or did badly. Well, by the time I met Nancy — she made me feel good from the first time I talked to her on the phone — I hadn't even laid eyes on her yet — she booked all my travel.

[GABE: Uh-huh.]

TOM: She had this great laugh and this flirty sense of humor, and she said, "We've been talking for weeks, I want to meet you already!" And I began to think, Why the hell not? What am I saving myself for? This hyper-critical woman waiting for me back home? Who looks at me with withering disappointment. All the time. This accusatory, how-could-you-be-so-thoughtless look. So, on one hand, there's this *delightful* woman who makes me feel worthwhile and there's this *other* woman, my *wife*, who makes me feel like shit. Who would *you* choose? *(Pause.)*

DINNER WITH FRIENDS
Donald Margulies

Scene: Here and now
Dramatic
Gabe (late thirties to forties), a man in love with his wife.

Here, Gabe explains to his friend, Tom, why he could never consider leaving his wife.

GABE: You don't get it: I *cling* to Karen; I *cling* to her. Imagining a life without her doesn't excite me, it just makes me anxious.

[TOM: *(Backing off.)* Okay . . .]

GABE: It all goes by so fast, Tom, I know. The hair goes, the waist. And the stamina; the capacity for staying up late, to read or watch a movie, never mind sex. Want to hear a shocker? Karen is pre-menopausal. That's right: My sweetheart, my lover, that sweet girl I lolled around with on endless Sundays, is getting hot flashes. It doesn't seem possible. *(A beat.)* We spend our youth unconscious, feeling immortal, then we marry and have kids and awaken with a shock to mortality, theirs, ours, that's all we see. We worry about them, *their* safety, our *own,* air bags, plane crashes, pederasts, and spend our middle years wanting back the dreamy, carefree part, the part we fucked and pissed away; now we want that back, 'cause now we know how fleeting it all is, now we know, and it just doesn't seem fair that so much is gone when there's really so little left. So, some of us try to regain unconsciousness. Some of us blow up our homes . . . And others of us . . . take up piano; I'm taking piano. *(Pause.)*

THE DREADED WORD
Galanty Miller

Scene: Here and now
Serio-Comic
Kroeger (twenties), a slacker.

Here, Kroeger rails against the world as it is presented to him via the cathode ray tube.

KROEGER: I was watching some protest in Iraq or one of those fucking countries. They were burning American flags. Don't these people have anything else to do? God I hate other countries. There are like, only three things people in other countries do. They either stand around protesting, they stand around shooting each other, or they stand around starving to death. Don't any of these people have fuckin' jobs?

[ANTONIO: *You* don't have a job.]

KROEGER: Yeah, but at least I occupy myself. I have a schedule. I watch TV. Nobody in these other places ever has anything to do. Is there one person in Iran who says, "You know what? I can't go out and burn U.S. flags today because I gotta get to the office." Does Iran even have offices? Or what about Africa? Does anybody ever say, "You know what, I can't stand around and pose for the UNICEF cameras today because I'm a dentist and I have appointments today." You would think one person in one of those countries would come up with the brilliant idea of buying a building and opening up a store.

THE DREADED WORD
Galanty Miller

Scene: Here and now
Serio-Comic
Dave (twenties), a young man searching for some meaning in life.

Here, Dave shares his philosophical musings with a bum he's encountered on the street.

DAVE: Sometimes I think having a family would be nice. But sometimes I don't. Sometimes I think having a steady job for the rest of my life and making a lot of money would be nice. But sometimes I don't. Like you said, I don't know where the finish line is. I wish God would just come down and tell me what to do. I wish he would say, "Get married. That's what success is. Have two kids, not one and not three but two." Whether I like the results or not, I just wish I knew what I was supposed to do, what the ending was. You would think God would do that when you're like eighteen or something. He'd invite you up for a beer and tell you what your purpose is. "Okay, Dave, here's what I want you to do. I want you to get your Masters degree, but don't go any further in school. Then I want you to keep your first job after school for about a year. Then I want you to keep your second job for the rest of your life." Life would be so much easier if God was more social. *(Pause.)* Do you believe in God?

THE DREADED WORD
Galanty Miller

Scene: Here and now
Serio-Comic
Antonio (twenties), a young man nursing wounded pride.

Unlucky in love, Antonio here does his best to put on a game face for his buddies.

ANTONIO: You know what, sure I'm depressed right now. I just got rejected. And I'll say things I don't mean, or that I won't mean a few days from now. But I'll get over it. And I'll move on and I'll meet someone else and I'll be happy. Or maybe I will try to call again. I don't know. But I'm just glad my life moves on, I can't stop it. I don't know if I'd want to freeze eight years of my life doing nothing. Dave, are you really happy going from woman to woman without any depth to any of your relationships? Aside from the avoiding commitment thing, you don't learn anything from all these people. Every date you've had this year is essentially meaningless in the overall structure of who you are, of your life. And Kroeger, so you get a job and it sucks. So what. You'll just move on to the next one, a better one, and if that one sucks, you can just go to another one. And if you never find anything you like to do, big deal, join the club. But in the meantime, a million other things will be going on in your life.

THE GOOD GIRL IS GONE
Dolores Whiskeyman

Scene: Here and now
Dramatic
Papa (thirties), a hard working man whose wife has left him.

> *When his wife leaves him to raise their two daughters alone, Papa refuses to admit that she's really gone for good. Here, he calls the police station for the umpteenth time to demand that they find her and bring her back.*

PAPA: How many times has a guy gotta call before somebody takes him serious . . . I did. I did fill out a report . . . Bender. B-E-N-D — okay . . . Public servants, my ass. Entire police department needs an overhaul . . . hello? . . . Case closed? How can the case be closed? My wife ain't here, is she? If she was here, the case would be closed but until she gets back, the case is STILL OPEN . . . Hello?? Hello?? Who is this? . . . Okay, sergeant, maybe you can talk some sense into — I know I did . . . I know that's . . . sergeant she's got two little girls here . . . what's that got to do with it? . . . she's missing! So what if she went on her own, I want her to come back . . . not a police matter? How can . . . well if the sanctity of the family ain't a police matter, then I DON'T KNOW WHAT IS!!
(Ginny covers her ears at first, then finally can't stand it and crawls under the table as Papa keeps talking, only quieter.)
(Overlapping.)
I been married to the woman for 15 years. For 15 years. You understand what 15 years is?? — Fifteen years worth of grocery lists, that's what 15 years is — 15 times 52 is — what is it anyway? 780 grocery lists, that's what it is. 780 trips to the grocery store, it's five thousand four hundred seventy six mornings of wakin' up next to the same woman . . . you get to know somebody that way, I'm tellin' you, and I know that woman, even if she went on her own she didn't plan to stay gone, she wouldn't a stayed gone and left these little girls here . . .

THE GOOD GIRL IS GONE

Dolores Whiskeyman

Scene: Here and now

Serio-Comic

Steve (thirty to forty), a doctor. A predatory male; ambitious but drug-addled.

Here, Steve the doctor riffs on health care, mental health and his residency.

STEVE: Who gets the heart, who gets the kidney. That's the great conundrum of our age. We can do the transplant — but we don't have the kidney. Pure medicine — pure medicine says everyone gets the kidney! But that's not reality, now is it? And the one thing you're going to learn from being in here — is reality. That's the key to mental health — being able to tell the difference between reality and fantasy. In fact it's really the only legal distinction. The law doesn't care really, whether you're happy or not — that's not what mental health is. Mental health is: Are you going to kill somebody because you think they're an agent of the Devil? Because if you are — then they lock you up here. But if you're just, mildly unhappy say — just functionally miserable — and you only occasionally THINK about swallowing Drano — but you never actually BUY any Drano — and you don't think anyone is the Devil and you show up to work on time and you don't take long lunches and you stay off the telephone and you leave your troubles at home — now THAT is mental health and THAT makes you a fully functioning human being regardless of the chaos swirling through your brain. So you see — it's all a matter of appearances. As long as you LOOK like you've got it together, then you do. Until you go crazy and shoot somebody, of course, but that's not our department. If we follow the universally prescribed course of treatment and therapy for someone with your condition, we're covered. Everybody knows you can't predict human behavior — although you can control it with the proper amount of Thorazine. Are you going to take that?

[GINNY: Don't I have to?]

STEVE: Is it you — the patient — who should decide the course of your medication and treatment? Or me, the doctor? Some guys would say, why do you even ask her that? You idiot! You're the one who spent four years in medical school. You went through the hellhole of your internship, you're the one who sucks up to arrogant attendings, who goes days on end without sleep — who spends every night praying to God please Jesus deliver me from this hellhole of a residency — all of which, you see, makes me, somehow, the moral superior of my patients, who didn't have the wisdom to go to medical school. That's the stimulant, right?

HEARTS
The Forward Observer
Willy Holtzman

Scene: The years following World War II
Serio-Comic
Donald (fifties), a WWII vet sharing his memories.

As Donald struggles to squeeze into his old Ike jacket, he shares some memories and bemoans his failing health.

DONALD: *(Gruffly.)* Ten-hut. Staff Sergeant Donald L. Waldman, 3rd Army, 71st Infantry Light Division, 608 Field Artillery Battalion, "B" Battery, Forward Observer. Service in two armies and seven corps. Advanced over 800 combat miles from the Ardennes in the Battle of the Bulge to Linz, Austria on the Czech border – the farthest point east of any U.S. fighting unit in the war.
(Grins.)
Thought I was Patton for a second there, didn't you? All that regular army "spit and polish" bullshit. I'll tell you about Patton — he would have made a helluva Nazi. What made him a hero? He was our Nazi. You can have Patton. I'll take Doberman.
(Bulges his stomach, juts his jaw in a comical underbite.)
Doberman. You know, the sad sack go-fer on the old Sergeant Bilko show? "Hey-up-hah! At ease, soldier." "Okay, sarge." My best impression. My only impression. You don't remember Doberman? Patton, you remember. The point is that somewhere between Patton and Doberman is Waldman. Come to think of it, I do a terrific impression of me. Here's me under fire for the first time in Belgium.
(Cowering, abject terror.)
Here's me crossing the Rhine.
(Daintily tiptoes.)
Here's me if the war went on another six months.
(Prone, dead.)
This is the Ike jacket I wore the day I came home. Hail the conquering hero!

(Tries to button the jacket over his stomach.)
Inhale.
(It's no use. He exhales.)
Fuck it — I'm throwing it out.
(Peels off the Ike jacket.)
To think this thing actually used to fit. With room to spare. Don't get me wrong — it's not like I pull it out every Veterans Day. Hell, I wouldn't be caught dead marching in one of those parades. I try it on from time to time. What, you never tried on the old high school letter jacket? You never tried on the old wedding dress? Not you, buddy, her! All I'm saying is each time there's less room. Like the thing is inhabited. Haunted. "The Jacket of Dorian Gray." Only it's in perfect shape, and I'm going to pieces!

So I'm not the picture of health. So the doctor says I've got a bit of a weight problem, which goes very nicely with my blood pressure problem, which wouldn't be caught dead without my heart problem. But dying? No such luck. My problem is living. My problem is outliving my secrets. My problem is this fucking jacket!

(Throws the jacket to the floor.)
I should've thrown the damn thing out years ago.

HEARTS
The Forward Observer
Willy Holtzman

Scene: The years following World War II
Dramatic
Babe (thirties), a WWII vet with a sleeping problem.

Even though the war is over and he's safe at home, Babe still can't seem to get any sleep.

BABE: Since the war, my definition of sleep has changed. The shooting stops, but the thinness of it all, the wakefulness . . . With the new baby, and all, I've become aware, I'm reminded of things not so long departed, memory things, Donnie. Things I meant to cast out, banish. Still there. The baby cries in the middle of the night, I'm already awake. The baby smiles, I cry. Some wires got crossed. Some gears, pedals. The brake is the gas, the gas is the clutch. It's hard to get from place to place in my mind, sometimes. I know, I know, life is good. We live in a clean, safe place. We're making healthy babies. We have houses, carports, rathskellars. This is what we fought for. We won! So why is this happening?
(Donald devours more candy.)
I can't sleep like a normal person. You can't eat like a normal person.

HEARTS
The Forward Observer
Willy Holtzman

Scene: The years following World War II
Dramatic
Donald (fifties), a WWII vet sharing his memories.

As a forward observer, Donald was first on the scene at the Buchenwald concentration camp. Here, he recalls his grim discovery in chilling detail.

DONALD: The guard towers are empty. Not a single sentry. The electrified gate is wide open. The driver wants to stay back with the jeep, "Maybe it's already liberated."

But I know better. What tells me? The smell. Good God, the smell. I know it from the battlefield, the bodies rotting in the April sun. There are no words to describe it. If there are POWs here, they are past liberating. I lower my rifle and walk.

Out of nowhere, they start appearing. Not army green. Stripes.

First a few, then a dozen, then hundreds.

I'm pulling Hershey bars from my pack, C-rations. All gone in an instant. Still, they keep coming.

I want to shout, "What are you? What have you become? How could you let them turn you into animals, more dead than alive? The stink of death is on you. How do I liberate the dead? Shame on you. Shame!"

(The voices stop.)

I fall between the ticks of a clock. I wander, the Forward Observer, wordless among worn, yellow stars and windowless barracks as silent as coffins. I blink back tears and my eyelids are like shutters, snapping incomprehensible pictures: a bloodstained meathook double-bolted into a reinforced concrete wall; a cast-iron furnace door still hot to the touch; an infinite knot of naked limbs; a windblown spiral of ash. Passover rewritten, undone.

I'm standing outside Barracks #39. A man staggers towards me, a tin of half-eaten C-rations in his hand.

Nothing is revealed. You don't even know who I am!

That you let them reduce you to this just to survive. I'm a fighter, a warrior!

How could you do this to yourself?

I'm one of you. I'm you. How could you do this to me?!

He sinks to the ground. The air hisses out of him like a leaking balloon, and he dies. I look to my left, to my right — they are dying all around me.

Why are you dying? You've been liberated. I risked everything to be here. Lost my way. Lost my best friend. Lost myself. Lost . . . to find you . . . to save you. I have come to Buchenwald! And you won't even save yourselves? Why are you dying? Why?

Got vet shtrofen! God will punish!

HUNGER
Sheri Wilner

Scene: A beach house in Nantucket
Dramatic
Adam (twenties to thirties), a man struggling to save the woman he loves from
 her own fears and desires.

> *When it seems that Diana prefers the company of a mysterious man who has
> appeared from the sea, Adam reveals how he used to lose himself as a child
> watching ships sail by.*

ADAM: I used to sleep on the couch by that window.
 (He points to it.)
That one. When I was a kid. And I'd watch the ships go by. I'd spot them
on the far left and I'd follow them all the way across until I couldn't see
them anymore. And I'd forget. I'd forget that I was in a house watching
a ship instead of actually being on the ship sailing on the sea. And when
I couldn't see it anymore — the ship — I'd feel so . . . disoriented. I
wouldn't know where I was or how I got into this body or how I'd ever
make it back on board. When another ship came, I'd be OK. But the times
when it took forever until another ship passed . . . when I'd wait and not
be either here or there . . . that's when I thought I'd never survive.

IN BERLIN
Jim Grimsley

Scene: Berlin
Dramatic
Walter (forty to fifty), a man trying to discover something new about himself.

When his younger lover leaves him, Walter travels to Berlin to visit Kurt, a man who arranges S&M scenes for discerning customers. Walter is paying Kurt a small fortune to arrange a powerful scenario for him to observe. Here, Walter remembers a childhood hymn as he prepares to enter Kurt's dark world.

WALTER: In my head I am singing this song.
(Sings a verse of I'll Fly Away.)
We sang it in church when I was a kid.
This little plank church on a country road
in Georgia near the Florida line
we sang it on Sunday morning and I thought it would be true one day
I would fly away
anything seemed possible
in a world where a man could ride a chariot straight into heaven without even dying
and for a long time when I was older I thought sex was like that
like I would fly away

But we also sang this song
(Sings verse of another song with submission reference.)
In those days I guess I only sang the words, I never understood
but now I'm older and I can hear the message
and I wonder if maybe I should change the way I think about sex to match that song

This is all in my head, all what I'm thinking, as if I were thinking out loud, but the truth is, I'm scurrying through Berlin like a worm, a frightened man in good shoes looking for a taxi stand and hoping he can pronounce the name of this street, in reality I am this small, scurrying thing scuffling through the clean streets, mindful to stay out of the bicycle paths, looking for a driver to take me to East Berlin, where the boys are waiting

There's power in the blood
we sang that too
but I'm not ready to think about that

When I get to the place it's just a building, just an apartment building, and there's nobody on the street, a broad street with a median down the middle, and I go into the door of the apartment building into this empty carriageway, completely dark, and I can't find the light switch for a while, and when I do it's one of those European light switches that gives you about five seconds to get where you're supposed to be, and I'm not, I'm still in the middle of that carriageway trying to find the stairs, because I already know there's no elevator, and the apartment, the studio, is on the fifth floor, so I fumble forward and I find it, the newel post of the stairway, and a step, and I begin to climb.
(Sings, softly, a verse of Power in the Blood.)
When I get to the door it's just a door, I ring the bell, somebody buzzes me inside, and there I am
(Lights rise on Kurt.)
But any one of those moments lasts a long time
I walk into a dark passage
a dim orange light is burning at the end
I am thinking, this is a strange place to have come to, a crumbling building in East Berlin, a place where people are stingy with the lights
and this man in leather standing in a doorway
waiting for me, I have made an appointment and here I am
on time.

IN MY HEART I KNOW I'M RIGHT

Galanty Miller

Scene: The Hereafter

Serio-Comic

The Angel of Death (any age), a supernatural entity suffering from ennui.

Here, a weary agent of God laments his choice of occupation.

THE ANGEL: *(Lying in bed.)* Back when I was alive, I very much believed in God. But I only believed in Him because if there was a hell then there had to be a God. And back when I was alive, I thought I would go to heaven. But I only believed in heaven because I figured as long as there was a hell, there had to be a heaven. Still, it was always about hell. It was about punishment and consequences and the whole underrated concept of revenge. I tried so hard in life to do the right thing. It wasn't always easy but I did it — I lived life the way I knew in my heart it was supposed to be lived. And I didn't care if there was an afterlife for myself. I only wanted there to be an afterlife for the millions and millions of other people who didn't live life the way I did — the bad people. I wanted them to die, and then for them to be told exactly why they were going to hell. I wanted them to have a chance to think about it for awhile, to wallow in their regrets. Then they would go to hell and get physically and emotionally tortured. Maybe not a very poetic way to look at things but that's what I believed and that's what I hoped for.

(The Angel stands up.)

I guess it's true that you should be careful about what you wish for because it might come true. But this didn't just come true, it was always true. What I always somehow knew in my heart was right. A lot of people feel things to be true in their heart, but usually they're wrong. That's because most people are morons and they're stupid and they're selfish and evil. Fuck them and fuck what they think about anything. Nobody thinks they're going to hell — even murderers rationalize their actions to themselves. Well there has to be justice in this world and every place else. There has to be punishment. There has to be some solace for me because of how I lived. And you're not a bad person if you believe in this punishment or even if you encourage it. You can even enjoy it if you want. I love when bad things happen to bad people. I love it. No amount of pain they suffer as a consequence to their actions is great enough for me.

(The Angel sits in a chair near the front of the stage.)

So as I sit here, and I do my job — this despicable job to which there doesn't seem to be an end — at least I know I'm doing what deserves to be done. And I have no regrets about that. So all the murderers are rotting in hell. And the rapists and the molesters, the thieves and the criminals — all wasting away. The people who lie, the people who cheat. The selfish, the hypocrites, the ignorant. I've sent them all away. People who are mean and cruel and violent, and people who . . .

(Long pause.)

(The Angel stands up.)

I was never chosen! I worked my way to where I was and to where I am. And I hate it! And the people who are so-called chosen are no better than any of the other losers who I hate. *(Pause.)* Sometimes I almost envy the mediocre. Imagine having no real conscious thought outside doing what you feel like. It must be comforting.

(Long pause.)

But who cares. Who cares about any of them. What, did you think this whole thing was about them? It never was about them. It could have been a guy who likes strippers or a guy who ignores his kids or a guy who beats up his wife or drinks and drives. Whatever. It never really mattered who I was gonna judge. They're all the same to me after awhile. No, this was always about me. It was always about righteousness and purity and . . .

(The Angel falls to the ground. He is lying on the stage.)

But whatever. I need to get out of here. I need this to end. I'm a prisoner. And even that no longer matters.

(Long pause.)

Because when it comes down to it, I could probably be happy if . . . *(Pause.)* there were better shows on TV and I could just find a decent cup of coffee.

LAST TRAIN TO NIBROC
Arlene Hutton

Scene: Kentucky, Late Summer, 1942
Dramatic
Raleigh (twenties), a young man with epilepsy struggling to find his way in
  life.

Raleigh suffers from epilepsy which has cost him a place in the war and on
the assembly line. When the young woman he loves, May, reveals that she dis-
dains his father because of his drinking and prefers the company of a pompous
young preacher, Raleigh reacts with anger and hurt.

RALEIGH: You don't know what being ashamed is.

[MAY: I feel very ashamed.]

RALEIGH: Ashamed is when you can't go off to war with your buddies. When
  you're going to be the only one left in town.

[MAY: *(Almost overlapping.)* I know that.]

RALEIGH: Ashamed is when you have the fits in front of your sergeant.

[MAY: *(Almost overlapping.)* I'm sure it is.]

RALEIGH: Ashamed is when you give up your own dreams to chase after something in a skirt and find out she's not worth running after.

[MAY: You're not talking about me.]

RALEIGH: Ashamed is when your new girl won't come to supper at your house
  because your daddy is a cripple.

[MAY: I said I was sorry —]

RALEIGH: Ashamed is when you run into that girl a year and a half later and
  you realize what a stupid mule-headed old rooster you've been for ever
  seeing something in her in the first place. Ashamed is having to come home
  to a dirt-poor farm and feeling guilty about taking care of your mama
  and your daddy. And instead of going off to war having to go to Detroit
  to stand fifteen hours a day on the line in a loud, sweaty dark factory.
  Ashamed is when the factory doctor tells you you got ep'lepsy.

[MAY: You preaching at me?]

  (He is having the very beginnings of very mild convulsions.)

RALEIGH: You better leave now. Better catch your train.

MAN MEASURES MAN
David Robson

Scene: Macedonia, near the Kosovo border. The recent past.

Dramatic

Yuli (forties), a Serb fighting to rid Kosovo of ethnic undesirables. A murderer and a rapist.

Yuli's band has just attacked, raped and killed in a Muslim village in Kosovo. Here, he shares his brutish insights into sex with a younger member of his group.

YULI: I've had better. These days, though, your choices are limited. *(Lights rise on Agim, center stage. He clutches his journal.)* How did you like her? Older, but not so bad, huh? Let me tell you something, boy — a bit of advice: You will see a lot of punks your age going for the young pussy — pretty common, actually. The young ones have those fine, strong bodies — supple skin. Ah! But when it comes to sinking your stick, the older ones have some things going for them. Give us middle-aged bodies some credit. *(Stops combing.)* Do not tell me she was your first. *(Begins combing again.)* My advice? Get what you can now . . . Where the — How could I forget my fucking toothbrush? Of all the things. Oh well, what is use of brushing your teeth without good close shave to go along with, eh? *(Brief pause.)* Ah! Good bread, warm pussy. And a little money in our pockets to boot. Not a bad day all in all. *(Brief pause.)* If you had not convinced me to let her go we could have kept her for awhile, brought her along with us — good for a few days, you know? I think she would have liked it. But no! Mr. Sentimental. *(Mocking Agim:)* "We have to let her go, Yuli. We have to let her go." *(Brief pause.)* Oh well, I am being hard on you, aren't I? You are good boy, but you need direction. Not all that unusual at your age. What are you now? Seventeen? Eighteen?

[AGIM: Almost twenty.]

YULI: Twenty? You have got a young face. That is what it is — a young face. Anybody ever tell you that?

[AGIM: you have.]

YULI: I have. Sure. Be thankful, because when you start getting the creases — jowls too — you might as well kiss sweet youth goodbye. People used to tell me I had young face, but look at me now.

THE MEMORY OF WATER
Shelag Stephenson

Scene: Here & Now
Dramatic
Mike (forties), a TV doctor who's just received some shocking news.

When Mike's mistress, Mary, announces that she thinks she may be pregnant,
Mike unhappily informs her that he had a vasectomy before he ever met her.

MIKE: Look. I know you want a child, I accept that. I know you're furious with
me for having a vasectomy —

[MARY: Five years and you never mentioned it, that's what I can't —]

MIKE: I don't want a child, Mary! I don't want a child. I can't want one just
because you do. Love and paternity aren't indivisible in my mind. When
I say I love you it means I like you, I want to be with you, I want to go
to bed with you, it means all sorts of things but it doesn't necessarily mean
three children and Sainsbury's every Saturday for the next thirty years —

[MARY: No, you've already got that —]

MIKE: I can't help what happened before I met you! You might not like what
I'm telling you, but I can't lie to make you feel better. I never wanted kids
in the first place. They happened and now I love them but I don't want
any more. It's not because I'm cold or selfish — at least no more than
anyone else is — it's that I feel sucked dry by what people need from me
— patients, Chrissie, the children. You're where I come to be equal, I
come to you because you're not asking to be healed. Some people aren't
paternal. It's not a crime, I'm one of them. If you're a woman and you
take care of your own fertility, nobody argues. Well, I've taken care of
mine. I didn't have a vasectomy because Chrissie's ill, I had it for me. *(Silence.)* But obviously, you know, if you *are* pregnant, I'll stick by you.

THE NEGRO OF PETER THE GREAT
Carlyle Brown

Scene: The Court of Peter the Great of Russia
Dramatic
Ibrahim (thirties), the adopted son of Peter the Great. African.

Ibrahim has been recalled to St. Petersburg from Paris by the Czar. As he makes the long journey, Ibrahim recalls the happiness he found in Paris as well as his love for Mother Russia.

IBRAHIM: Please. This is difficult enough. I can't stand good-byes. Usually I just go away. I was going to write. I hadn't the courage to tell you all until now. But I wanted to thank the Countess for her pure, spontaneous soul. Her passionate devotion and her boundless tenderness towards me, I shall never forget. When I first came to Paris, Korsakov and I only slept in carriages, going from one ball to the other. You see, I was born in Abyssinia, a land where the night air is too sweet to sleep in, and my brother Korsakov and I, we are Russians, and we Russians can dance forever. But it's difficult being a foreigner. You stand out. Everyone immediately thinks they know who you are. And once they see you, they will never accept anything else about you other than what they think they see. It was only in Countess Leonora's salon, that I found friendship, and a place to be myself, and not Le Negre de Czar. I will not dishonor my self with tears. These memories must last me for a long time. Perhaps forever. Memories to carry me on the long journey ahead. Memories to carry me through memories. Through France, the Austrian Netherlands, the Holy Roman Empire, Saxony, Poland, and from Prussia, to the Russian frontier. And then on to St. Petersburg, a journey as long as it took to cross nearly all of Europe. It's just turning autumn now. The thick woods of birch trees along the river Neva are wearing their winter shadows, and in the orchards at Oranienbaum, the apples are falling to the ground. St. Petersburg. In the heart of my homeland, holy mother Russia, where they will welcome me like a prodigal son. Bring me the rest of my baggage footman.

NO. 11 (BLUE AND WHITE)

Alexandra Cunningham

Scene: Suburban Connecticut
Dramatic
Brian (sixteen to eighteen), callous and sardonic.

Here, an emotionally bereft young man reveals his secrets for wowing the young ladies.

BRIAN: No, you couldn't, you bone, who would do that? The point is to establish that it's *her* and *you* against everyone else, all right? It's called divide and conquer, heard of it? If you don't want to know then don't fucking *ask* me, okay? She'll say, I thought the lax players just partied all the time. You say, Well, I come to these things because my friends throw them and it is kind of a team spirit issue and also I do occasionally enjoy partaking of the Brotherhood of the Grape, but after a certain point the scene grows old and I'd really rather just be home. *Writing.* And she'll go, Wow, really, what do you write? And you go, oh, just some *poetry,* it's really nothing. And she'll say it's not nothing, can I hear one, you're totally wowing her with the killer one-two of simultaneously being really sensitive to literature and also fucking built like a *warrior,* and so you lean in real close and probably take her hand and hold it to your heaving chest so she can see what it would have been like to have been in a clinch with an actual *Viking,* and you let her have it.

No! With a poem. What the hell is the matter with you? You let her have it with a *poem.*

Wanna hear the one I've been using lately? Listen up, scrote.

Oh terrible darling,
How have you sought me,
Enchanted and caught me.
See now where you've brought me —
I sleep by the roadside and dress out in rags.
Think how you found me;
Dreams wash around me —
The dew of my childhood, and life's morning beam;

My heart that sang merrily while I was young
Swells up like a billow and bursts in despair.
And the wreck of my hopes on sweet memory flung
Are all that is left of the dream.
You'll burn in my heart till these thin pulses stop;
Your fragrance I'll drain
To the last brilliant drop.
The dream of my longing and wreck of my soul
Dancing, inspiring
My wild blood to firing
Oh terrible glory
Oh beautiful siren
Come tell the old story again.

. . . I'm telling you, they hear that and like my Dad says about his old
Camaro, "She starts right up!"
Love and death. They're the keys, pal. They make it a whole new ball-
game out there, and I do mean *ball*game.
No, I didn't write it. But who the fuck's gonna know that? Nobody knows
anything anymore anyway, and even if they did, what are the odds that
some dippy gash you meet at Eric Hanford's wake-and-bake is gonna be
the one who does.

SHERIDAN
David Grimm

Scene: The city of London, the end of the eighteenth century
Serio-Comic
Richard Brinsley Sheridan (forty to fifty), a playwright.

Sheridan has given up writing to pursue pleasures of the flesh and philosophical indolence. When the idealistic young poet, Lord Byron, takes him to task for having abandoned his art, the older man makes the following reply.

SHERIDAN: Oh, how all you eager aspiring writers love to spout ideals — How this is wrong and that is wrong and this is how it should be. But tell me, lad, what happens when you reach your summit — When you get what you wish for? All these hopes and ideals — What then? What happens when you wake one day and it's all there in your hand — be it a successful play, or a seat in government, or even love? What happens when you see the awfulness of the fact that reality can never live up to your dreams — That every striving leads to disappointment — That the world is a lump of shite. You see, I once believed as you do. Oh yes, I was full of the hope and anger of youth. Looking at you reminds me too much of what I once had. Looking at me, you're seeing your future. So look carefully, George, and tell me — What's the fucking point?

SHERIDAN
David Grimm

Scene: The city of London, the end of the eighteenth century
Dramatic
William Pitt (fifty to sixty), Prime Minister of England.

> *The king of France has just been arrested and Europe is on the verge of revolution. Here, Pitt awakes from a nightmare and endeavors to calm himself as he dresses.*

PITT: You step into the sun and at first the glare is enough to blind you — Committees, depositions, legislation, policies foreign and domestic, constituencies demanding to be heard. All around, the savage buzz of history unfolding in your blood. It is overwhelming — Like a fever. Avoiding history is avoiding one's own breath. In my nightmares, the world is cold steel awash in a sea of red. I fight. I fight. Ours is a country of infinite symbols — Stonehenge — The Magna Carta — The Chair of Kings sat in by William the Conqueror. These are the bindings of our national spirit. They must be upheld. My administration, like history, is built on strength. On the symbols that have shaped and conquered. Strength is a simple beast. It lives on a diet of other people's fear. History is infinite but fickle. My government is definite and driven. History doesn't give a damn what choice you make so long as you make it.

SHERIDAN
David Grimm

Scene: The city of London, the end of the eighteenth century
Dramatic
Richard Brinsley Sheridan (forty to fifty), a playwright.

Here, the melancholy playwright laments the happiness in his past with his young friend, Lord Byron.

SHERIDAN: Sadness? *(Laughing.)* It's happiness one must forget. Memories of pleasures past have more venom in their sting than any deep inflicted wound. My youth was near delirious! A fairy book of charm and light and certainty. *(Silence.)* Have you ever experienced beauty, George? A beauty so intense and so unbearable it pains the heart to look upon? There are no words for it. No words that I could ever pen. I see her, you know. Eliza. Usually, it's just the train of a gown turning a corner. Or the tilt of a hat, just so, from behind. I'll think I've forgotten and be walking down a street and there she is in the folds and flutters of a lady's fan. My breath catches. I run up. I look. It's never her. And then I'll know once more that she is buried in the damp cold ground. She was my gem and I tossed her in the mud and there's no forgiveness in the world for that. Oh, what a mawkish parody of man I have become. I will confess, I've thought of putting pen to paper once again. I find myself wondering what it would be like to stand in Parliament and speak with deep conviction as I once did. But could my small and hollow words make any difference when I've lost what I believe? Now all that's left are the motions and gestures. What if there is nothing beyond them? What if there never was? What if it's all been emptiness behind a fancy show — A wicked play of words with no meaning and no heart?

SHERIDAN
David Grimm

Scene: The city of London, the end of the eighteenth century
Dramatic
Richard Brinsley Sheridan (forty to fifty), a playwright.

After half a carafe of wine, Sheridan remembers the quiet moments in the theater he shared with the woman he loved.

SHERIDAN: Every Saturday night, after final curtain, we'd collect the candle ends — The hardened pools of wax on floors — The long and stiffened streams on curtains would be scraped off in a bucket — And then laughing, giddy, young, and thinking we knew better than the best of them, we'd run the buckets down the mills and have them melted into new ones. Always at four in the morning when the dew came — Always when the long and lonely shadows played across the empty cobbled streets — Always waking the candlemakers from sleep or lovemaking. Now the seat-cushions — the curtains — the creaking old wardrobes — Corsets and bonnets and mirrors and papers — A floor-board in the hall David Garrick carved his name on — The last time I ever made love to you was on a stairway which is now burning. The candles are melted, Eliza. All the wax is scattered.

SIDE MAN
Warren Leight

Scene: Here and now
Dramatic
Clifford (thirties), a man remembering his father.

Clifford's father was one of the last great jazz sidemen. Here, he remembers watching his dad play and mourns the loss of a great era in American music.

CLIFFORD: When he's up there, blowing, he's totally in touch with everything that's going on around him. Ziggy bends a note, he echoes it instantly. A car horn sounds outside, he puts it into his solo, or harmonizes under it, a second later. I used to wonder how he could sense everything while he was blowing, and almost nothing when he wasn't. Now I just wonder how many more chances will I have to hear him blow. If I have kids . . . These guys are not even an endangered species anymore. It's too late. There are no more big hands, no more territory bands. No more nonets, or ten-tets. No more sixty weeks a year on the road. No more jam sessions 'til dawn in the Cincinatti Zoo. When they go, that'll be it. No one will even understand what they were doing. A fifty-year blip on the screen. Men who mastered their obsession, who ignored, or didn't even notice, anything else. They played not for fame, and certainly not for money. They played for each other. To swing. To blow. Night after night, they were just burning brass. Oblivious.

SLOE GIN FIZZ
David-Matthew Barnes

Scene: Here and now
Dramatic
Marco (twenties), Latino. Sensual, desirable and never intimidating.

Marco has spent his life in denial of his attraction to men. When he meets Christopher, all bets are off. Here, he bravely confronts Christopher with his feelings in a declaration of freedom.

MARCO: I hate my life — and I've hated it for as long as I can remember. But I was getting by — I was good at pretending that I was happy. I was playing the role perfectly. And then, one day — two months ago to be exact — I'm at work — a job that I have to force myself to go to everyday — and I thought it would be like any other day. Bullshit with the guys, flirt with a couple of girls — keep everything safe. But then in walks Christopher — the new guy — all smiling and smelling good and showing interest in me and my feelings. And all of a sudden, it all made sense to me — the lies and the covering up and the denying — the fucking denying — for all of my life. Can you understand that? I have been lying for my *entire* life — but in you walked with the truth and the challenge — I saw it in you the first time that you spoke to me — you had what I had always wanted — freedom. Then I realized that I was attracted to you. I had to accept the fact that I wanted another man, that I desired him. Every second of every fucking day, I think about you — *constantly.* I think about what it would be like to hold you and touch you and kiss you and make love to you. I think about what it would be like to spend the rest of my life with you. Christopher, I came here tonight — because this is my last chance. I want my freedom — and I want it with you.

SLOE GIN FIZZ
David-Matthew Barnes

Scene: Here and now
Dramatic
Christopher (twenties), eccentric, quirky. Slightly effeminate and always graceful.

Marco has just come out to Christopher and declares his feelings. Here, Christopher expresses his sadness for the fact that we live in a society when men feel as though they have to pretend to be something they're not just to get along.

CHRISTOPHER: Gay men are the worst when it comes to this whole theory of "acting straight." It makes me sick.

[MARCO: But you don't care what people think. It's easy for you. I mean, with you, almost everyone can tell that you're gay.]

CHRISTOPHER: That's because confronting is better than conforming, Marco. I don't care about ridiculous expectations put on me by men. I am who I am and if someone doesn't like the fact that I cry at sad movies or that I like to slow dance or that I empathize with the emotional suffering of women, then fuck 'em. This is who I am. I like being a guy and I've never worn a dress in my life. If I want to be flamboyant — it's my right. If I want to be dramatic — then allow me to shine. It doesn't make me any less of a man. If I don't want to spend my life in a gym, pumping iron and popping steroids, hoping that I'll be thin enough or tan enough or big enough to capture the attention of some sleaze fuck barfly on a Saturday night in a dimly lit shit hole dance club — that's my decision. If someone meets me and because of the way I walk or talk or the way that I enter a room — they assume that I sleep with men — that's their own damn assumptions — not mine. I'd rather be me — imperfections and all — than to become something that other people want me to be. Just because a man is masculine doesn't make him any more desirable or attractive — if he's an idiot, he's still an idiot — usually it just means he has a bigger ego and a lot less intelligence. The fact that you feel that you have to act a certain way to survive in this world, it's the saddest thing I have ever heard. You are who you are, Marco. And I think you are beautiful, just the way you are.

STANDARD TIME
Naomi Wallace

Scene: A holding cell
Dramatic
Working-class Man (nineteen), a young man who has just murdered his girlfriend.

Here, a troubled young man does his best to explain why he shot his girlfriend.

WORKING-CLASS MAN: I wanted her car because I needed to steal because I wanted *(Flips the coin, catches it.)* money because money is — yeah, they say — power and power is a garden, is a tree that never stops, is a field you can't get to the end of and I never had anything beautiful in my life. *(Flips the coin, catches it.)* But her. Flip a nickel. Catch it on your tongue. *(He does so.)* It's got a tang; that was her mouth.
(He spits the coin out into his hand, studies it a moment.)
And Tally's mouth made me think on money. Always there but not there. You could touch it but you just couldn't keep it. Every time I opened my hand it was gone. The money. The money I didn't have and her mouth, well, it was hers and it went where she went.
(Lets the coin drop.)
I couldn't keep track of it.
We were seventeen. Tally's car was the only thing that could stop and go in our town, and when Tally was mine it was our car together. It was a wreck but we rode it. Didn't have a backseat so we didn't need one. We threw down a sheet of plastic and piled it with dirt to keep the rear low so we could floor it. And the wind from the open windows took ahold of our throats and made us gag with the thrust of it. In through our mouths and out through our ass, at 85 miles per hour, blasting us clean.
(Uncovers the saddle, sits astride it.)
And one night Tally stole a saddle from a saddlery barn on the Pop-side of town and we strapped it to the roof of her car and while she drove, I rode, with the wind brushing my teeth into the kind of smile I couldn't make on my own. I was the Marlboro Man and I swept over that high-way like I was sweeping plains while the other cars scattered like cattle in front of my wheels.

We were just kids. Kids. You know what that means? But we still couldn't stop being junk. That's what they called us in our hometown: J-town junk. And we didn't have a future cause we didn't have a dime but when we were driving we were nothing if not cold, hard cash, banking on the next turn to give us a spin and send us into America. Because that's where we wanted to be. Inside America. Where the sky is red and the heart is blue with the boast of it. And where your pockets are full. Yeah, where your pockets are full.

But that's where we couldn't get.

(Gets off the saddle.)

And then one day, it could have been any day just riding around wasn't enough because even the Marlboro Man needs some spare change. And my ass was getting sore from the speed of it all and down below me Tally was rolling up the windows 'cause it had started to rain and then one, two, three, the colors just washed out of me and I was an idiot on a wet saddle, tied to the top of a wreck and the grass was starting to grow up through the dirt in the backseat of the car.

And then. Well. And then that's how the story goes if it goes at all. I took a breath or two. Tally must have done the same and then we weren't. Girl-friend and boyfriend. She turned around. Took a step. I missed one and it was over. And we passed the way days pass and it was another season by then, somewhere between August and waking up alone and that was it: She was gone. Her mouth was gone. The money none of us had was gone.

Time passed. That's what they say. Time passed. And I got to thinking that maybe it wasn't time passing but me, and I didn't even know it.

Days and months and pieces of things, they kept on passing. And every time I looked in the mirror it was her mouth I saw on my face, instead of my own. But when I touched it, touched myself, she was gone.

And so one night, it could of been any night, I needed her car. These are the facts: I went to her house. I hadn't been there in months. I said: Give me your car. She wouldn't let me have it at first. Then. Well, then she did.

The order. Of how it happened. Well, that was out. That's been out ever since, but when I said give me the car she just said: *You used to say my name like whiskey, like a light switch. Like a key.*

I said: I need the car. Tally said: *You would cover me in leaves up to my neck; you would never leave me.*

I said: This isn't about you and me. This is about ignition. This is about contact and speed and I need the car to get there by midnight. It's a lot of miles to drive but it's just up the road and the map's between my eyes and I know I can get there.

Tally kissed me then. Her mouth was cold like a piece of the river. And for a second I remembered: the books we'd opened at school, what we'd wanted for our lives, how a door swings open before it swings shut. And then she said. Tally said: We're already dead when I showed her the gun. And she was right.

I never got to the Five Star — You're going the wrong way! — Never got to the steal. She wouldn't let me. She wouldn't let me drive — You're going the wrong way! — She drove the car out into a field. *(Quietly.)* You're going the wrong way.

We were parked now just a few feet from the river. It had started to snow. It was August and there's no such thing as snow in August in our town and there never has been. But it started to snow. Tally got out of the car. I stayed inside. I watched through the windshield. She threw the keys into the river. And they were gone. I remember. I remember thinking. How big that car was when I sat inside it without her. How it would never move again. And all I needed was a little piece of cut metal, a thing that small was all I needed to turn the whole thing over, to start it up again. These are the facts: I got out of the car. Tally was standing there looking at the river like it was going to look back. She was covered in snow. I came up behind her. The snow all around us. The snow passing all around us like time and we stood still. I wiped the snow from my mouth but I couldn't feel my mouth. I touched my face but I couldn't feel my face. And I kept touching my face, trying to get the feel back into it. Tally, she said: *Yes.* Tally, with her back to me, she couldn't even see me behind her. She said: *Yes.* I wasn't touching her. I was touching myself. But she said: *Don't stop touching me.*

And then I didn't know anymore. I just had no idea. I stood there. Stood there in that spot like I'd been standing there all my life. In front of me the snow covered her hair. She raised her hand to brush the snow off her hair and I felt her hand on the back of my head. She wasn't near enough to touch me but I felt her hand on the back of my head. And I just didn't know anymore. I said I love you and I pulled the trigger.

I didn't want her dead. I didn't want. Her dead. How many times do I have to say it? I wanted to get there. I wanted to get there and lay down and rest with a big, hot sun inside my chest and never be wanting again. *(Beat.)* I didn't want her dead. I just. Wanted the car.

(He slowly, gently turns the saddle onto its back so that it lies upside down. He moves away from it and turns away. Then he turns back to look at the saddle, lying on its back on the empty stage.)

Those are the facts. Those are the facts of love.

SYNCOPATION

Allan Knee

Scene: New York City, 1911

Dramatic

Henry (forties), a meat packer who dreams of becoming a ballroom dancer.

When his dance partner asks if he's Jewish, Henry makes the following reply in which he reveals a familiar immigrant's story.

HENRY: Catholic? No. No, I'm not.

I'm a Jew.

[ANNA: I thought so. You seem like a wanderer.]

HENRY: Forty-two years. I'm not very religious though. I oughta be. I think of it sometimes. I work for a kosher butcher. We've gotta wear yamulkas — even in the ice houses, where the meat is stored.

I came to America when I was eleven. I worked first in a glass factory. I cleaned out the ovens. It killed the spirit. The last few years I've been involved with the radicals of Rivington St. Very vocal men. They too kill the spirit . . . The first time I truly came alive I heard Adeline Patti sing at the Academy of Music. It was an unbelievable experience. She had a voice that only angels could have matched. I didn't sleep that night. I couldn't get her out of my mind. Something touched me here. Sometimes even an organ grinder's music fills me with joy.

THE THREE GREAT LOVES OF CHRISTOPHER J. TOMASKI

Patrick Gabridge

Scene: Here and now
Dramatic
Chris (twenties), a young man mourning the death of his sister.

Here, Chris contemplates joining his sister in death, hoping to find the freedom he imagines she's found.

CHRIS: And suddenly it's not such a big step. It requires only a small motion. Slight pressure. The glass is very sharp. Press a little harder and the skin breaks, but it's not enough to cut the vessel. The vein lurks, beneath, waiting. In case you ever make up your mind. Push a little deeper.
(He presses the glass into his wrist, and holds it still.)
Probe. Find it. For a second, it rolls, a last tease, avoiding. But it's clumsy, not fast enough to avoid the glass. It takes only an instant, and you're in. In. In. Now is not the time for second thoughts. Once the action has begun, it must be completed. What you have now is a pinprick. The blood stays blue, until you find the strength to draw downwards. Strength of will. Now is the moment to wish for a razor. A razor is the right tool, but a shard of glass will serve. Draw along the wrist, then wait.

[CHARLOTTE: You'll be happy.]

CHRIS: I can almost not comprehend the wait. The wait. How did she stand it? Thirty years, of preservation, of making sure that my skin stays intact, and now I have the power to undo. I am the one. The responsible party. The one.

[CHARLOTTE: Join me.]

CHRIS: I'll have my own secrets. But first there is an act of will. A final act of will.

[CHARLOTTE: To open and close a door. It's simple.]

CHRIS: It's simple. It is not as hard as it should be.

THE TIME OF THE CUCKOO
Arthur Laurents

Scene: Venice
Dramatic
Di Rossi (forty to fifty), a man searching for love.

When he encounters Leona, Di Rossi becomes attracted to her. Here, he makes his feelings known.

DI ROSSI: You will never never find romance by being romantic. Never! Yes, I am using the right words. In English! I now very well what you wish. You come here, you ride in gondola, and you sigh: Ah Venice! So beautiful, so romantic! Ah, these Italians! So lyrical, so romantic, such children! And you dream: he is young, handsome, rich, witty, brilliant. A gondola of his own. A duke, or a count at the very least. And — unmarried. Well, I am a shopkeeper. Not handsome. Not rich, not young, not witty, not brilliant. No title: no gondola. And not unmarried. But, Miss Samish, I am a man, and I want you. But you? "It's wrong, it's wicked, it's this, it's that." You are a hungry child to whom someone brings — ravioli. "But I don't want ravioli, I want beefsteak!" You are hungry, Miss Samish! Eat the ravioli!

[LEONA: I'm not that hungry.]

DI ROSSI: We are *all* that hungry! For what do we live? Believe me, when there comes a moment out of time, something sympatico between two people — big small, middle-sized but *something* — you must take a chance on it. *(A moment.)* The noise in your head is so loud, Miss Samish. Be quiet. Let it happen. I want it to happen.

TOO DIRECT
Jeff Goode

Scene: an audition
Serio-Comic
Kris (twenties), an awkward auditioner.

Here, Kris enters the audition and becomes a bit too direct with the director.

KRIS: Hi.

You probably don't remember me.

I mean, of course you don't, why would you?

But I was at a show you did, like, jeez, a year ago.

A friend of mine — Do you know Casey?

(Tiny pause, no response, move on.)

Right anyway. It was her idea.

I think she worked on it maybe, or she works here?

(Tiny pause.)

Never mind, doesn't matter. But so that's why I was here.

And they had that thing afterwards where everybody was just hanging out, and so that's where it was.

(Looks uncomfortable.)

Can I just — ?

(Climbs down off the stage.)

I hate being onstage.

But I heard you were having auditions and my friends were like "Go, go, you have to do this."

And so I don't know if this is weird or . . .

No, it is. It's weird, I know. It is, it's weird.

But the thing is — Can I just say one thing?

(Moving a little closer to the director.)

I don't know if you remember this, but there was this guy, the lead guy, you were taking to, big guy, I don't know his name.

And I don't know what he said or what you guys were talking about . . .

But you just went off on him.

You were just "And this, and this, and this, and this!"

And he was like, completely, had no idea.

And everyone was like, . . . wow.

You were just so . . . Confident.

You were like . . . on fire with it. It was amazing.

And I was just "Who IS that??"

And I know this is stupid, and I know this isn't what you want to hear right now while you're doing all this, I know you're busy. But I'm not an actor, so I don't know how I'm ever going to even get a chance to even BE here just to say . . .

(Looking the director in the eye.)

I would give anything. To be here.

Right now.

Like this.

With you.

TOUCH
Toni Press-Coffman

Scene: Here and now
Dramatic
Kyle (thirties), a man in terrible pain.

Kyle's wife, Zoe, has been murdered by street thugs. Here, Kyle describes Zoe's last agonizing moments as they were told to him by her killers.

KYLE: I talked to each one of them separately. Each one could have said no, but each one agreed to speak to me. Which I didn't understand at first, but now I think it was Zoe. Zoe was smiling. Zoe was telling me I am dying, Kyle. It's what my life is now. I'm dying. *(Kyle stops, and closes his eyes and breathes. He opens his eyes.)* The first one said no, he didn't notice she was smiling. He was young, still a teenager. *(Beat.)* She said if one of them would stay there with her until she died, she would like that. *(Beat, he can hardly say this.)* She would be grateful. *(Beat.)* Zoe hated to be alone. This kid was spooked by that. He told me he didn't know why, but he grabbed her purse and ran with it. He had killed before, but he didn't want to be there when Zoe died. So the other one stayed with her. He was closer to her age — mid-twenties. *(Kyle closes his eyes and breathes. His measured breath becomes more shallow, becomes panting. He opens his eyes.)* When he came into the visiting room, he sat down, rigid, and fixed his gaze on me. He didn't speak. *(He takes a deep breath, like he did then.)* I asked him if he noticed she was smiling and he said yes. *(Pause, like he's waiting for more, like he did then.)* I asked him was she scared and he said yes. *(Beat.)* But as she faded, she seemed less and less so. He leaned toward me, and said her smiling made him furious and he asked her what the hell was so funny. She said, "Funny?" *(Beat.)* He sat back again, straight in his chair. And he stared. He looked — right — through — me. *(Pause.)* I asked if she spoke my name. He said no. He said he didn't want to piss me off but she was "one weird chick." Because as she lay dying, she mumbled something about the stars. *(Kyle closes his eyes and breathes. He opens them abruptly.)* GODDAMMIT, KEEP YOUR EYES OPEN. KEEP THEM OPEN. *(Beat.)* She died. *(He breathes, but his eyes are open. He becomes frenetic.)* I spoke to her murderer. I said to her murderer, whether or not there is life in some other galaxy, Zoe's huge heart notwithstanding, regardless of Triton's beauty, no goddamn matter how much she loved me or what shape Sagittarius is, she fucking died. He said you're crazy too, buddy. I banged the telephone on the Plexiglass separating me from him. I said did you touch her? *(He closes his eyes, opens them.)* Keep them open, Kyle. *(Beat.)* Did you touch her while she was dying? And there it was. He flinched. He looked at me. DID YOU FUCKING TOUCH HER? *(Beat.)* She — uh — she reached her hand out to me, he said. She reached for me. *(Beat.)* Yeah. I let her touch me. *(Kyle stops, cries, breathes, waits.)* I said —. I said —. We met in my physics class.

THE TRESTLE AT POPE LICK CREEK
Naomi Wallace

Scene: A town outside an American city. A jail cell.

Dramatic

Chas (fifties), a jailer obsessed with his son's tragic death. Well-meaning but lost in the past.

Fifteen-year-old Dalton has been arrested for the murder of Pace, a complex young woman who at one time was Chas's son's girlfriend. Here, Chas approaches Dalton in his jail cell in a first effort to break the boy's silence about the alleged crime.

CHAS: On break. Thought I'd sit it out with you. The other guy, across the hall. He's looking for grass in his cell. Thinks he's a moose. Could be some other herbivore but every now and then he lets out this call but it sounds close enough to a moose. Yesterday, a bug. Some kind of beetle, I think, with huge claws. He used his arms like pinchers. Opening and closing them. Opening and closing. For hours. Wayne was leaning in to give him some grub and the next minute he caught Wayne around the neck. Almost choked him to death. While I was prying him off he's making this sound. A beetle sound, I guess. Sort of like . . .

(Chas makes a "beetle sound.")

Self respect: gone. Was the manager of the Plate Glass Company. A real Roosevelt man. Good to his men, though he laid them off. Then his head went pop one day and he started breaking up the plant. Glass everywhere. Wrecked half the place. Even the WPA says close it down. No one needs glass these days. Might want glass but they don't need it. Mr. Roosevelt, I say, want to buy some glass? Them up high's got the money to want. They don't have to go by need. What kind of a beetle was it, you think? Big pinchers. Opening and closing. How'd the visit go? I know your folks. Nice people. Sorry to hear your Daddy's still out of work. But who isn't? Well, I'm not. I'm still here. Could be somewhere else, like Spain shooting some whatyoucallem, but I might get killed and then bein' here looks better. I had a boy like you. You must have known my Brett at school. Big fellow. Fast runner? Moose's easier to identify. Distinctive. My break's about up. So what do you think, kid? How many years do you think you'll get? Or will they hang you? When they hang you the last thing you hear is your own neck break. And if you got a real thick neck bone, a strong one, a young one, then it takes a while to break clean through, sometimes hours, and all the while you're dying you're hearing it snappin' and crackling and poppin', just like a stick on a fire. So what do you think?

THE TRESTLE AT POPE LICK CREEK

Naomi Wallace

Scene: A town outside an American city, 1936. A jail cell.

Dramatic

Chas (fifties), a jailer obsessed with his son's tragic death. Well-meaning but lost in the past.

By spending time with Dalton in his cell, Chas has become consumed with unhappy memories of his son, Brett, which he here shares with the nearly catatonic Dalton.

CHAS: Now him over there, he doesn't know who his mother is. A turtle doesn't consider those things. Want to know how I know he's a turtle? *(He demonstrates, impressively, a turtle, moving its neck in and out of its shell.)* I know what you're thinking: could be a goose. I thought of that. But a goose doesn't do this — *(He moves his head slowly from side to side, then cocks his head to one side, opens his mouth and eats.)* A goose doesn't eat like a turtle. How you feelin, boy? What're you thinking? Still won't talk. Still won't talk. But they got it on record when they brought you in: Yeah, I killed her. That's what you said. Why didn't you lie? They don't have a witness. Four words. Just four words: Yeah, I killed her. But won't say why. Won't say how. What kind of a game are you playing? Well, they'll find out. They know about kids. I had a boy your age. Couple of years older than you. *(Beat.)* To think. He was just a kid like you. Scared of nothing. Yeah. Scared of nothing cause you are nothing. Half of you kids wanting to kill, the rest wanting to die. Ordering death likes it's a nice, cold drink and you're going to suck it down in one gulp and then get up and walk away from it. Right. Kids. Just want to eat, fuck and tear the ornaments off the tree. But only if you don't have to get out of bed in the morning to do it. The whole damn country's going to hell cause of your kind. *(Beat.)* You should have killed your own self instead. That's what they say. *(Beat.)* I loved my boy Brett. But I never could figure what he was. Something kinda small. Like a wheel, maybe. Something that spins in place in the dark. He had a gap in his heart. He was empty. I know; I was his father. Sometimes he'd ask me to embrace him. *(Shrugs.)* He was my son. *(Beat.)* So he'd be here, in my arms, sniffling like a baby. But there was nothing. I was holding him. He was in my arms. But it was like holding onto. Nothing. *(Beat.)* What's it feel like to be that empty? *(Begins to take off his shirt.)* I'm going to have to hate you, I guess. There's not much choice.

(Chas stands over Dalton. Dalton is shivering and does not respond. Chas puts his shirt around Dalton.)

CHAS: I'll bring you home some dinner. You've lost weight. Hard not to in here.

THE UN-XMAS STORY
Jeff Goode

Scene: A hillside

Comic

Shepherd (twenty to sixty), a man who has been visited by an angel of the Lord.

Here, a disgruntled shepherd describes his fateful encounter with an angel.

SHEPHERD: Okay, stop me if you've heard this one. Angel walks into a bar. Angel of the Lord. Glory shone round about, the whole deal. Walks into a bar. Bartender goes, "You just fly in from the coast?" Angel goes, "Yeah, how'd you know that?" Bartender goes, "Your arms look tired." But seriously, so this Angel — Angel of the Lord, right? — looks around this bar. Little dive bar, 'bout a mile out of town. You take the south road, you can't miss it. Looks around the bar, the Angel. Looks around. What do you think? Table in the corner. *Shepherd.* Just sittin' there. Minding his own business. Isn't hurtin' nobody. Angel walks up to him. Angel of the Lord. Walks up to the table. Glory all around. Shepherd is like, "Now what?" Angel turns around, motions toward the door. Boom! Heavenly host. Praisin' God in the highest, peace on earth. You know the drill. Bartender goes, "Hey! Let's see some I.D." Angel goes, "Aw, c'mon!" Bartender goes, "Let's *see* some *I.D.*" So the host is all over at the bar going through their wallets. And it's all, like, out-of-state and "this doesn't look like you" and "left mine at home" juvenile kind of shit.

[ANGRY VOICE: *(Offstage.)* Hey!]

SHEPHERD: So the Bartender's thinking, "Sorry I asked." And the Angel is like, to the shepherd, "Whaddaya say we get outta here?" And the Shepherd is like, "What?? I just got here. I got a table. You know how hard it is to get a table in this place?" And the Angel is like, "Yeah, but . . . I gotta talk to you a minute." And the Shepherd is like, "So talk." And the Bartender goes, "Hey! This one's under age." And there's this host — one of the host — can't be more than 15, swear to God. Busted, totally. And the Angel's like, "No, wait, no wait." And the Bartender's like, "You think I'm playin'?" So the Angel, to the Shepherd, is like, "You wanna step outside?" And the Shepherd is like, "Oh, so now you're gonna kick *my* ass?" And the Angel is like, "No, no, it's not like that." And the Bartender is like, "Out! Out!" And he's chasin' this little host around the bar. Got a broom. Chasin' the little guy around. And he's running into tables, knocking over chairs. Complete mess. And then he ducks behind the bar. Which you *do not do*. Bartender is like, last straw, goes ballistic, "That's it! Everybody out!!" *(Shepherd looks irritated.)* . . . So now I lost my table.

[ANGRY VOICE: *(Offstage.)* Get on with it!]

SHEPHERD: I'm just sayin'.

[ANGRY VOICE: *(Offstage.)* All right, already!]

SHEPHERD: So this Angel — Angel of the Lord — goes to the Shepherd. Shepherd still a little pissed.

[ANGRY VOICE: *(Offstage.)* All right!]

SHEPHERD: Goes to the Shepherd. "Fear not." *(Shepherd rolls his eyes.)* Goes, "I bring you good tidings of great joy." Shepherd is like, "Yeah, it better be good." Angel goes. "For unto you is born this day in the City of David, a Savior, which is Christ the Lord," right? And the Shepherd is like, "Yeah? So?" And the Angel is like, "Whaddaya mean, 'So?' " And the Shepherd is like, "What do you want me to do about it?" And the Angel is like, "The Savior, man! You gotta check it out." And the Shepherd goes, "I'm on my break." "You're on your break?" "I'm on my break. I stopped by for a quick drink. I get a table at the bar. I *had* a table at the bar. Now I don't got a table at the bar. I got 20 minutes before I gotta be back at the herd because I picked up a double from Joab because he needed off to take care of his taxes. So now I'm gonna be up all night with the sheep." And the Angel goes. "Don't worry, I'll watch the sheep."

THE UN-XMAS STORY
Jeff Goode

Scene: A hillside
Comic
King (forty to sixty), a Wise man from the east.

This king's been on the road a while as he here relates to Joseph.

KING: You know how hard I worked for this?

[JOSEPH: Nuh uh.]

KING: Three years! For three years I've charted stars, planets, phases of the moon. Went through decks and decks of tarot cards. Sacrificed God knows how many perfectly good goats, just to crosscheck my findings with the entrails. Oh and God, the tea leaves! *There's* six months of my life I wish I could have back.

[JOSEPH: What can you tell from tea leaves?]

KING: Nothing! The whole field is complete horseshit. I don't know what I was thinking. The stars are cosmologically linked to the four elements. There's a basis in science, at least. But what does a cup of tea know? But it just goes to show how badly I wanted this. How desperately I wanted to be the first. Or one of the first. The top five at least. To be at the first to meet Him. To welcome Him into this world. This God-forsaken desert world.

[JOSEPH: Yeah. World kinda sucks.]

KING: But now, after coming thousands of miles out of my way . . . Because, could he be born in the East and save me a trip? Nooooo! It's gotta be Bethlehem. City of David, house of David, line of David. *And* it's in the middle of winter! So after tracking this stupid star across mountains and deserts. And more mountains and more deserts. And then this last desert which is the one that really pissed me off.

[JOSEPH: Yeah, you don't want to come in from the East. You gotta take the first exit around to the South.]

KING: I go through all that, just to be the first. Not even the first, because Gaspar figured it out, too. And he told Balthasar. And whoever that other guy is. *(Confidentially.)* But I don't think he knows. I think he just saw us packing and was like, "Dude! Road trip!" So he came along. So, okay, maybe I'm third if I'm lucky. So we're almost here after three years and 3000 miles, right? And the *day* before we get here, this fucking Angel just goes and tells everybody! Everybody in town knows. The place is a madhouse. There's Shepherds running around looking for him who don't know shit. They didn't have to do trig equations. They didn't have to design and construct their own primitive telescope out of bamboo. They didn't have to translate vague Jewish prophecies from the original ancient Hebrew. And I think they stole my camel. Or maybe not. I shouldn't accuse. But I got down for one minute to take another reading on this stupid star and I can't because the town is packed, and everyone's bumping into me, because they're all running around looking for him, and I can't get a good read. So he could be anywhere. He could be in any one of these barns. And I turn around . . . Gone. My camel's gone. And Gaspar and the guys are gone. And I got Shepherds rubbing into me. And I *know* some of 'em are doing it on purpose. Because anything's gotta look sweet after you've been doing the menage á flock for three months. And now my agoraphobia is starting to kick in. And I just had to get out of there.

WHEN THEY SPEAK OF RITA
Daisy Foote

Scene: Tremont, New Hampshire
Dramatic
Jimmy Reeves (nineteen), a young man in love with his best friend's mother.

Here, Jimmy awkwardly declares his love to Rita.

JIMMY: Don't you say that. Why do you think I come over here all the time?
I can't stop thinking about you. When I'm at work with my Dad, when
I'm at my house, when I'm in my truck. When I'm sleeping, when I'm
sleeping I'm dreaming about you. And you're a star in my dreams, Mrs.
Potter, just like you're a star when I'm awake, a bright, shining star.
(A beat.)
It's your family, they're the ones making you feel this way. They don't ap-
preciate you. I see the way Warren yells at you, I see it and I can't stand
it. It's all I can do not to punch him out.
(A beat.)
I love you, Rita — I love you.

80

HEARTS by Willy Holtzman

Copyright 2000 by Willy Holtzman

HUNGER by Sheri Wilner

Copyright 1997 by Sheri Wilner

84

Reprinted by Permission of the Author

Contact: Patrick Messer and/or Kevin Urrutia, All-Star Talent Management, 1-800-566-8428

STANDARD TIME by Naomi Wallace

Copyright 1999 by Naomi Wallace

Reprinted by Permission of The Joyce Ketay Agency

Contact: The Joyce Ketay Agency, 1501 Broadway, Suite 1908, New York, NY 10036

SYNCOPATION by Allan Knee

Copyright 1998 by Allan Knee

Reprinted by Permission of the Author

Contact: Melissa Hardy, Bret Adams, Ltd., 448 West 44th Street, New York, NY 10036, 212-765-5630

THE THREE GREAT LOVES OF CHRISTOPHER J. TOMASKI by Patrick Gabridge

Copyright 2000 by Patrick Gabridge

Reprinted by permission of the Author

Contact: Patrick Gabridge, 14 Linwood Street #3, Roxbury, MA 02119, *www.gabridge.com*

THE TIME OF THE CUCKOO by Arthur Laurents

Copyright 2000 by Arthur Laurents

Reprinted by Permission of the Author

TOO DIRECT by Jeff Goode
Copyright 2000 by Jeff Goode
Reprinted by Permission of the Author
Contact: Jeff Goode, 1501 Brentwood Lane, Wheaton, IL 60187, *Jeff-Goode@aol.com, www.jeffgoode.com*

TOUCH by Toni Press-Coffman
Copyright 1998 by Toni Press-Coffman, all rights reserved
Reprinted by Permission of the Author
Contact: The Peregrine Whittlesey Agency, 345 East 80th Street #31F, New York, NY 10021

THE TRESTLE AT POPE LICK CREEK by Naomi Wallace
Copyright 2000 by Naomi Wallace
Reprinted by Permission of Broadway Play Publishing
Contact: Broadway Play Publishing, 56 East 81st Street, York, NY 10028

THE UN-XMAS STORY by Jeff Goode
Copyright 2000 by Jeff Goode
Reprinted by permission of the Author
Contact: Jeff Goode, 1501 Brentwood Lane, Wheaton, IL 60187, *Jeff-Goode@aol.com, www.jeffgoode.com*

WHEN THEY SPEAK OF RITA by Daisy Foote
Copyright 2000 by Daisy Foote
Reprinted by Permission of Helen Merrill, Ltd. on behalf of the Author
CAUTION: Professionals and amateurs are hereby warned that WHEN THEY SPEAK OF RITA by Daisy Foote is subject to a royalty. It is fully protected under the copyright laws of the United States of America, and of